SWIMMING AND DIVING

AMERICAN NATIONAL RED CROSS
WASHINGTON, D.C.

AMERICAN RED CROSS

SWIMMING AND DIVING

Prepared by the American Red Cross

WITH 67 ILLUSTRATIONS
UNDER-WATER PICTURES MADE AT SILVER SPRINGS, FLORIDA

DOUBLEDAY & COMPANY, INC.
GARDEN CITY, NEW YORK

PRINTED IN THE UNITED STATES OF AMERICA

PREFACE

In the last analysis safety in the water depends upon swimming skill and the ability to take care of one's self. Safety devices may not always be available in an emergency, and persons skilled in rescue may not always be near the scene of a water accident. If a person can swim reasonably well, however, he will always have the ability to make his way to safety or to remain afloat until he is picked up. A person who cannot swim, on the other hand, when he gets into deep water, is going to drown within a minute or two unless someone is nearby to help him.

This is the reason why the American Red Cross considers its program of instruction in swimming the most basic or fundamental part of its Life Saving and Water Safety program. Without skilled swimmers there could be no lifesaving training program because one has to be a strong and capable swimmer before he can acquire the skills of swimming rescue. Furthermore, no person should attempt to become skilled in the use of canoes, rowboats, or small sailboats until he has acquired enough swimming skill to take care of himself in case of accident.

Since it was started in 1914, the Life Saving and Water Safety Service of the Red Cross has recognized the need for and has provided swimming instruction as a part of its water safety program. Because, however, there was such a very large number of non-swimmers in the beginning, it had to concentrate its effort at first on teaching beginners by mass instruction methods. By 1934 it had become evident that this was not enough because a considerable number of those so taught never seemed to get beyond the beginner stage of swimming development. All too often it seemed they had learned to swim just well enough to get into trouble.

In 1934 work was begun on a program of graded swimming instruction courses which would lead a non-swimmer progressively and by orderly steps from the beginner level of swimming to the point where, if interest prompted to go that far, a person could become an advanced swimmer. Teaching methods were critically examined, refined, and altered to the point where the pupil could derive maximum result from his effort, and the teacher from his method.

In 1938 this textbook, *Swimming and Diving,* was published after 4 years of intensive research and study. Its acceptance was immediate because the bathing public had long needed a book of this kind. For 18 years it has been used as the authoritative text for all Red Cross swimming instruction programs in this country, standing well the tests of time and use. Instructors and pupils alike have absorbed the knowledge and acquired many of the skills described herein.

...atic skill in the United States has
... 1914; it has risen more rapidly
...s still, however, much to be done.
...ports and recreation is continually
...re are even now millions of persons
... in and on the water who either
...ll or swim so poorly that they are
...ger of drowning. The task of teach-
...e of people is a great one, but it can
... It requires only a considerably in-
... of Water Safety instructors and
...eople to learn. To this great task of
...rning the art of swimming this book
is rededicated.

Ellsworth Bunker

PRESIDENT,
THE AMERICAN NATIONAL RED CROSS

The level of aquatic skill in the United States has risen steadily since 1918; it has risen more rapidly since 1918. There is still, however, much to be done. Interest in water sports and recreation is continually increasing and there are even now millions of persons seeking recreation in and on the water who either cannot swim at all or swim so poorly that they are frequently in danger of drowning. The task of reducing this multitude of people is a great one, but it can be accomplished. It requires only a considerably increased number of Water Safety instructors and willingness of people to learn. To this great task of teaching and learning the art of swimming this book is dedicated.

President
THE AMERICAN NATIONAL RED CROSS

ACKNOWLEDGMENTS

The Swimming and Diving Textbook has been written by Carroll L. Bryant and is a companion volume to *Life Saving and Water Safety*. Mr. Bryant was a member of the staff of the Safety Services for 27 years and served as national director of the Water Safety Service for 7 years. He is at present director of the Office of Publications of the national organization. His long training and experience in the fields of physical education, recreation and athletics have singularly fitted him to write on the subject of swimming.

Tribute is paid, also, to the small group of Safety Service representatives, chapter directors, and selected Water Safety instructors who tested by actual use, the content of the book before it was published. Their findings were of great value.

ACKNOWLEDGMENTS

The Swimming and Diving Official Rules has been written by Carroll L. Bryant and is a companion volume to the Swimming and Diving Safety. Mr. Bryant was a member of the ... of the Safety. Six years for ...

CONTENTS

CHAPTER   PAGE
I. INTRODUCTION TO SWIMMING   1

II. LEARNING HOW TO SWIM   15

III. ELEMENTS OF SWIMMING   45

IV. STYLES OF SWIMMING.   98

V. OTHER FORMS OF SWIMMING   149

VI. DIVING   178

INDEX.   267

AMERICAN RED CROSS
SWIMMING AND DIVING

CHAPTER I

INTRODUCTION TO SWIMMING

As practiced by man, swimming is an art. Fish, amphibia, water-fowl, and practically all quadrupeds are either born with the ability to swim, have instincts which enable them to acquire swimming ability very rapidly, or employ a form of locomotion on land which with little adaptation is suitable for making progress through the water. If man possessed anyone of these characteristics or, even if he had six inches more of neck and six inches less of thigh, there would be no art to swimming. No swimming methods would have had to be devised; no one would have to be taught how to swim; nothing would have to be written or said about it. Everyone could, as the need or desire arose, simply enter the water and swim away just as most animals can and do. But in so doing man would have foregone an experience which has enriched him not only physically but mentally as well. Furthermore, he would have missed completely the opportunity to become that which he is, one of the most amazingly versatile of all creatures, in the water.

It is true that man is very badly handicapped by structure and habit when he enters the water. His normal position for locomotion on land is upright and he walks or runs by thrusting against the ground with a relatively small area of the foot.   An erect position in the water is a poor one for making progress not only because of the resistance offered but, more important, because of the narrow margin of buoyancy possessed by the average man.   The specific gravity of a human being is so nearly that of water itself that the average man, when suspended motionless in the water, finds that he submerges to approximately the level of the eyes.   Since in this position his mouth and nose are below the surface, he is quite unable to breathe without making some move to lift himself a little above his normal flotation level.   If, in this position, he attempts to employ the same movements he uses in walking on land, the thrust of the small area of the foot against such an elastic medium as water can barely hold him in a position in which he can breathe, and any sustained progress is out of the question. Even such natural and instinctive movements of the arms as pawing and pressing downward against the water, produce little result either in keeping a person's head above water or in moving through it.   So, since man's natural position and locomotive movements cannot serve him in the water with any degree of success, other positions must be assumed and different types of movements employed.   Such positions and movements have been discovered and developed, many of them in use to this day being as old as man's experience in the water.   Born of reason, nurtured by constant experiment and practice, and passed along from generation to generation, they have come down through the ages as a singularly simple, but none the less, important and fundamental physical art.   It is doubtful if anyone has ever learned how to swim in any

manner other than with the crudest of animal movements, without some foreknowledge of this art.

It is literally true that with his acquired art of
swimming, man is one of the most, if not the most,
versatile of all living creatures in the water. He is
limited, of course, in the distance he can swim, the
depths to which he can descend, the speed he can make,
and even the length of time he can be immersed. In
these things, fish, amphibia, even some mammals can
far exceed him. Man excels in the water rather in the
great variety of positions, swimming movements,
maneuvers and directions he can assume, employ, or
take. He can swim on the front, on the side, on the
back, at the surface or beneath it. He can swim forward, backward, even sidewise with ease. He has the
ability to somersault either forward or backward, or
to rotate on his long axis like a rolling log. But above
all, he has and can use many varied and different
movements of his limbs to sustain and propel himself
in the water.

Aside from his capacity to reason things out and his
singular, imitative ability by which he learns from
others, man has one physical asset which accounts in
large part for his versatility in the water. This is a
set of swivel or ball and socket joints in his shoulders
and hips which permit a wide range of movement in
the arms and legs. Swimming animals are limited by
their mechanical structure to far fewer patterns of
swimming action.

Because man differs so markedly in structure and
mechanical movement from other forms of animal life,
there is little or nothing that he has been able to copy
from them in developing his art of swimming. While
he has evolved many swimming stunts and given them

animal names, such as seal-diving, alligator-roll, muskrat-swimming, porpoising, and many others, they are only simulations of effects. The physical action employed to accomplish them is usually radically different from that of the animals he seeks to emulate. The dog and the frog have often been cited as examples among animals, the swimming movements of which may be copied by man for certain styles of swimming. One crude style of elementary stroke is called the dog-paddle almost universally, yet only in the pawing action of the arms and hands does it in any way resemble the swimming action of the dog, and even that is modified. If the legs were employed as the dog uses his hind legs, practically no progress would be made for any distance. Another classic example from nature of erroneous pattern is found in the development of the breast stroke where all through history learners have been told to imitate the frog in using the legs. Indeed, the breast stroke kick is commonly termed the frog-kick. Yet only in the negative or recovering portion of that stroke does the human swimmer even remotely resemble the frog. By thrusting backward against the water as the frog does with his widespreading webbed foot, man would get little result for his efforts.

So there is really little or nothing that man has been able to borrow from the rest of the animal kingdom in the development of his own peculiar art of swimming. Slowly and patiently over the centuries he has had to discover his own principles and methods. To swim, man has had to learn from other men, and such variations and improvements in styles of swimming as have been evolved through the years have of necessity had to be based on what had gone before.

Through the years there has been developed a literature on swimming and, more recently, photographic reproductions, both still and motion, of the elements of the art. Teaching methods have been devised for people to acquire the art more readily. It is not necessary for anyone to go through the whole painful "trial and error" method of learning how to swim so long as there are now swimmers to imitate, books on swimming to read, pictures to look at, and instructors available to teach.

Pre-history of Swimming

What prompted man to take to the water is a matter of pure conjecture, yet from what is known of the pre-history of man and from our present day knowledge of primitive peoples, it can be said that the three fundamental motivating forces were economic necessity, comfort and preservation of life in the face of danger. Of these three, economic necessity was, undoubtedly, the dominating force. The myriad forms of marine life must have been from the very first a great source of sustenance for man. In tropical and sub-tropical regions, seeking to escape the discomfort engendered by extreme heat, man must have discovered early in his experience that immersion allayed that discomfort; and over all the inhabited earth man has used the water from earliest times as a refuge from fire, animals or men. It can be said also, that man may have learned to swim as a result of accidental immersion in deep water but it is doubtful if his experience in his struggle to regain the land ever prompted him to repeat it, or others to follow his example. Other motivations may be cited such as that of cleanliness, bathing as a religious rite and even sport but as unique developments they must have come much later.

Where man first entered the water and learned to swim must also be a matter of conjecture but here a theory may be advanced which can be supported by considerable evidence. It is probable that the inhabitants of lands bordering warm shallow seas were the first to develop ability to swim. The conditions found under such circumstances must have been most conducive to swimming. Warm shallow lagoons teeming with marine life with barrier reefs and bars which excluded large and dangerous sea animals must have induced man to turn to them. There are exceptions, of course, but where these conditions are found today, there will be found people who have most universally and highly developed the art of swimming from times immemorial, the most notable example of such conditions and development being found in many groups of islands, especially in the South Seas. Wading, reaching and groping for food in shallow waters undoubtedly preceded actual swimming and paved the way for its development.

When it comes, however, to the actual development of swimming strokes it is not necessary to guess what the process was. Every self-taught swimmer in the matter of learning to swim demonstrates clearly the evolution of it. His motivations are the same as those of the first beginners; namely, to keep from drowning, to make progress through the water and to sustain the effort to limits consistent with need and comfort.

To swim, man learned that another position had to be assumed, that artificial movements had to be made and that all negative movements had to be made gently in order that they should not impede his progress. Swimming developed on these bases. The long process of development was on a "trial and error" basis and through the ages it must have been painfully slow. Little structural change was possible but possibilities of mechanical adaptation were almost unlimited. And so, by constant experiment and by simulation, man learned which movements would propel him and which would retard his progress; which would bear him up and which sink him and how these movements could be co-ordinated for the best effect. When co-ordinations were established which were somewhat efficient and suitable for others to imitate, swimming as an art, was born.

History

Of the art of swimming prior to the year 1500 there is but fragmentary evidence. Ancient literature contains numerous references to swimming indicating that it was well-known to the ancients and in common use among people of many races. Tales of great feats of swimming prowess are recorded in the sagas of Scandinavia, in the first bit of English literature known, the epic poem Beowulf, and in the classics of Rome and Greece but in every case the feat itself and not the means of its accomplishment is described. Prior to the sixteenth century no one, apparently, thought it necessary to describe the strokes used or any method of teaching; or, if he did, his work was not considered worthy of preservation.

The earliest form of swimming stroke probably was what Ralph Thomas in his splendid and authoritative work on Swimming chooses to call the "human stroke." It is described as an alternate arm thrust forward and downward with the recovery made under water and an alternate up and down thrash of the legs with the thrust being delivered in the downward movement by the top of the extended foot and the front of the shin.   This stroke is in common use today especially among self-taught novices and is better known as the "dog-paddle," though only in the stroke of the arms, does it resemble the action of a quadruped. This stroke was suitable for covering short distances but because of its limitations it had, of necessity, to be adapted to other conditions and requirements.   The process of adaptation, therefore, brought about the evolution of swimming strokes as they are known today.

Certain peoples, notably in the Slavic group, evidently found the original style of swimming suitable for their needs and never developed any other type of stroke for universal use.   The fact that they inhabited the great central plains of Europe, intersected by numerous streams, but away from large bodies of water, may have checked any such development. However, it is true that even up to modern times, this crude form of stroking was still in use in many parts of the world.

Primitive races, in temperate and torrid climes, where the art of swimming was pursued extensively, almost without exception developed the hand-over-hand method out of the original stroke, if the accounts of early travelers and present day evidence are to be believed.   This adaptation consisted almost wholly of recovering the arms over the surface and using a combination of lateral squeeze with the up and down motion of the legs.   With this stroke it was possible to move more rapidly and to meet more variant water conditions. What influenced this development can be but a matter of pure conjecture for the most part. A minimum of clothing, especially on the upper body, pursuit by sharks or other dangerous sea animals and the parallel development of the light craft (canoe) with the use of the paddle, undoubtedly played a definite part. The necessity for speed would bring the arms out of water in recovery, almost involuntarily. The example of the use of the paddle and of hand paddling when the paddle was lost, the canoe capsized or filled with water, must have had a definite influence upon the evolution of this stroke, as well. Incidentally, it may be remarked of this, that early explorers reported that the North American Indians were hand-over-hand swimmers and it is interesting to note that when this stroke was brought to England in 1873 by Trudgen, it was promptly labelled the "Indian stroke."

Visual evidences of the early use of this stroke are not lacking and through them can be traced an unusual motive and a still more unusual method of developing it.

In the Nimroud Gallery of the British Museum are a series of excellent bas-reliefs depicting swimming figures, which were discovered in the Nimroud Palace in Assyria by Sir Austen Henry Layard. These bas-reliefs are assigned to a period about 880 B.C. Most of these are of military motive, depicting scenes of battle or assault in which the soldiers are shown crossing streams. In most cases they are shown swimming with the aid of a mussuk (an inflated goat or sheep skin) which is used in the Near-East even to this day.

With this clasped beneath the breast with one arm, they are pictured using the vertical kick and an over-

hand stroke with one arm. Of considerable signif-
icance, however, are a number of figures in which it is
apparent that either through being pierced with an
arrow or being discarded, the mussuk is not in evidence
and the soldiers are swimming an unmistakable hand-
over-hand stroke. It may reasonably be supposed,
therefore, that military necessity motivated swimming
development among the highly civilized Assyrians and
that the mussuk was used first as an aid for crossing
streams. Later it must have been used as a swimming
accessory because of the weight of fighting impedi-
menta and not because of inability of the soldiers to
swim.

That this style of swimming should extend to the
peoples inhabiting the lands of the Eastern Mediter-
ranean area was to be expected since through many
invasions of Assyria, the military leaders of Byzantium
and Greece could not fail to take cognizance of its
value. At any rate, it is known that the hand-over-
hand stroke was used by the Greeks and, later, by the
Romans. As evidence, there is the so-called "Coin of
Abydos," a coin preserved in the British Museum,
depicting Leander swimming a very graceful hand-
over-hand stroke across the Hellespont while Hero,
standing in her tower with a lighted lamp, indicates the
way. This is dated A.D. 193. On still another frag-
ment, a painting found on a wall of a ruined house in
Pompeii, there is a depiction of Leander swimming the
hand-over-hand stroke, proving definitely that the
stroke was known to the ancient Romans.

During the Middle Ages from approximately 500 to
1500 A.D. swimming produced scant literature or
visual evidence in painting and sculpture that has been
preserved. While undoubtedly people did swim, until

the sixteenth century there is no source of information as to the strokes employed. Then, in the European literature of the time, began to appear a few treatises on swimming and, it is of interest that they gave the breast stroke as the one most commonly employed, indicating that in northern Europe this stroke was well established and had been in common use for many years, if not for centuries. The Germans, Scandinavians, Dutch and English were apparently foremost in its use as they produced the earliest and most comprehensive description of it.

How the people of northern Europe evolved the breast stroke from the universal "human stroke" is not known but a little conjecture can be hazarded that may have some plausibility. It would appear that there were two motivating forces in the arm portion, the weight of the heavy clothing of northern climes or armor (not necessarily metal), and the parallel development of the use of the oar for propelling boats. In the first instance, the water-soaked clothing would by its very weight make the hand-over-hand stroke impractical and in the second case, the example of parallel pulling, wide-sweeping oars would have been ever present. Although the frog is mentioned in the earliest literature on the subject as an example of how to use the legs, it is doubtful if the first leg strokes were slavish imitations of frog movements. It is more plausible to believe that the drawing and widespreading legs followed the example of the arms and were incorporated more easily into the co-ordination of the stroke. The frog was mentioned in this evolution probably, simply to cite an example in nature.

From this point the people of northern Europe went through the process of evolving a series of swimming strokes, turning from the breast to the side and the back and finally culminated the science with the over-arm side stroke used extensively in England in the middle nineteenth century. At this point when, because of the introduction of competition, speed became a factor of greater importance the hand-over-hand stroke came, thus belatedly, to Europe. It was introduced first by J. Trudgen in 1873, who learned it from South American Indians and because of his remarkable speed with it at sprint distances, it soon caught the public fancy but the trudgen stroke that was soon to be so popular became but an adaptation of the overarm side stroke to the new over water recovery of both arms. It was not until much later that the true hand-over-hand stroke with the vertical thrash of the legs was brought to Europe and America from Australia.

In America, as stated previously, the earliest explorers and settlers found among the Indians some who swam a hand-over-hand stroke. As a matter of fact the chroniclers of that time mention no other method of swimming as being used by the Indians. Such swimming as was done by the early white inhabitants of this country, however, would have been in no other styles than those common to the countries of their origin.

In the middle seventeen hundreds, Benjamin Franklin, an excellent swimmer himself, turned his attention to the art of swimming as it was then known. While he did not evolve anything new, he did throw some light on such problems as the specific gravity of the body in water and the use of arms and legs in the breast stroke. Furthermore, he gave an easy method of proving to one's self before actually learning how to swim, that the water will support a person of average buoyancy.

It is interesting to note that swimming in the United States has had its greatest period of development within comparatively few years. Peculiarly, it gained its impetus by means of a competitive motivation. The great increase in competition has caused Americans to seek styles of swimming and refinements of stroking movements that would produce ever greater speed over measured distances. Unfortunately, the list of competitive events has been narrowed down to only three methods of swimming, free-style, back stroke, and breast stroke. Free-style meaning "go as you please" is now restricted to only two styles of swimming for varying distances, namely, the crawl and the trudgen-crawl. In competition, the only stroke used on the back is the back or dorsal crawl. Even the breast stroke under the pressure of a demand for greater speed, is fast losing its classic style as more and more competitive swimmers are recovering the arms over the water in what is known as the "butterfly breast stroke." If the sole measurement of efficiency in swimming is that of speed, then undoubtedly these strokes may be called the most efficient of all since they serve to drive swimmers most rapidly through the water. But if such factors as utility, endurance, energy output and ability to swim easily and well without special training or constant practice, are considered, then there is something to be said for the classic styles of swimming. At any rate, this motivation has produced within a very few years three distinctly new styles of swimming, the American crawl, the dorsal crawl, and the butterfly breast stroke, and refinements of these strokes have been numerous.

In fast swimming, the United States has shown the way to the world and swimmers of other nations have not been reluctant to follow. In fact, by further refinement of method some of them have actually moved ahead of their original leaders.

What the trends will be in the future in the world of swimming cannot be foreseen but certainly this evolution of speed strokes and styles of swimming will have a marked effect upon the swimming of all the people. Out of them will surely come more effective and better ways of moving through the water, for everyone.

Down through the ages, man has sought to evolve newer and more efficient ways of swimming. Undoubtedly, individuals and even whole peoples evolved strokes far in advance of their time which were subsequently lost because their use did not become universal. Many methods of stroking were tried and discarded as ineffective and it is peculiarly interesting to note how few are the styles of swimming that have survived.

It seems now that man has experimented with every form and every combination of movement possible within his structural limitations, and has used every conceivable motivation. It would appear that any changes made in this novel form of locomotion will be but further refinements of methods already in use. Yet, who can say that someone with a new motivation or a new mechanical principal will not devise a new style of swimming tomorrow that will change the whole trend of swimming. Such things are possible.

What is now known about swimming must serve for those who would learn and be the basis for further experimentation. What comes after can be added to and embodied in man's experience in the water.

CHAPTER II

LEARNING HOW TO SWIM

It is possible for one to learn how to swim by his own effort. This can be done by imitating swimmers, by following the simple directions of any number of published methods from the printed page, or under the crude instruction of self appointed untrained teachers. It is a fact, however, that fundamentals are more easily learned and that progress is made more rapidly under skilled instruction. Over and above all that, however, the beginning swimmer is *safer* under the watchful eye of a trained instructor, a factor of considerable importance in the first stages of learning how to swim when the beginner is venturing into a new and, to him, often unknown element.

With or without a trained instructor, however, the non-swimmer should have a pretty thorough understanding of what plan he will follow to learn how to swim. Furthermore, he should be sure that he is going to be safe while he is learning. At organized bathing places and in tanks his efforts should be confined to those areas reserved for non-swimmers. In all other waters an area of shallow water should be sought in which there are no holes or sudden "step-offs." Likewise the non-swimmer should avoid waters where there are strong currents and hidden menaces such as snags, rocks, or channels. The bottom should shelve gradually and if the area is protected by natural or artificial boundaries which limit range and provide for reasonably calm water, it is still better. The learning process should not be undertaken alone or merely in the company of another non-swimmer. The presence of a swimmer or better, of a person trained in life saving, is fundamental to the safety of the beginning swimmer. A safe place in which to learn and someone to aid if something goes wrong are vitally essential because a near-drowning experience in the early stages of learning either greatly inhibits the learner's progression or quite discourages him from continuing.

Entering the Water.—When a non-swimmer enters the water for the first time, considerable adjustment has to be made both mentally and physically to the new element. Here is a new experience quite unlike anything he has ever had before. The water is cool, much cooler than the bath water he is accustomed to and its contact with the skin produces mild shock. The muscles contract almost involuntarily, the skin tingles, breathing is noticeably less regular and requires a distinct effort, and the pulse quickens. As the learner gradually submerges the body either by wading outward or by crouching, two things become noticeable; first, as the chest is submerged, it requires more effort to breathe because of the pressure of enveloping water and second, when the whole body is submerged, buoyancy develops and there is a sensible loss of weight. The exhilarating effect upon the mind is readily apparent; many persons laugh, scream, or shout at contact with the water and a beginner class of small boys or girls is frequently a veritable bedlam. It is, quite apparently, fun to get into the water and with the fun element the learning process should begin.

Before immersing the whole body, if the depth of the water permits, the non-swimmer should wade in up to the knees, then to mid-thigh depth. This is the time to kick and splash and to scoop up water with the hands and dash it over the face, the back of the neck, the chest, and the arms, gradually getting wet all over. Later he may sit down on the bottom and as the water rises to chin level, the learner gets used to the pressure of the water on the chest. It takes but a few moments for the breathing to become adjusted and settle back to normal. The muscles which may have become tense at the shock of cold water begin to relax and the learner begins to feel that it is "not so bad after all."

Then, a number of little play activities are tried to help get the "feel" of the water. Placing the hands on the bottom behind him, the learner may tilt the body backward and note how easily the legs rise from the bottom and seem to float. If the back of the head is laid in the water, not only does it give the ears their first submersion but the whole body tends to rise. The learner may then roll to the side and onto the front and begin little experimental kicking movements. With legs outstretched behind him, he may walk along the bottom on his finger tips. He can stand up and sit down repeatedly. Later, in company with a swimmer, life saver, or instructor, the non-swimmer may wade out into chest-deep water and submerge to the chin, trying to lift the feet off the bottom momentarily. All of these activities are perfectly natural ones; most of them are the things that most people do when they get into the water for the first time. They are something more than mere fun, however, for in doing them the non-swimmer unconsciously is performing a set of experiments from which he will learn

Fig. 1.—First adjustment of non-swimmer to water.

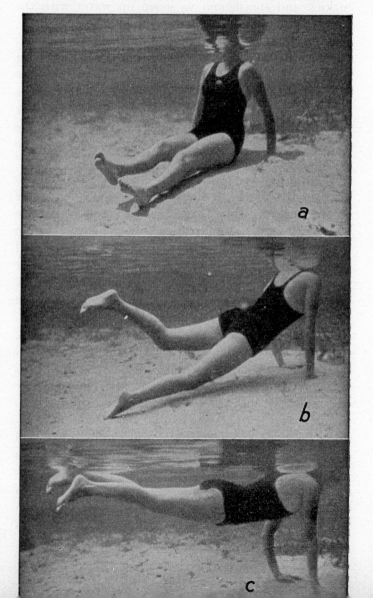

a great deal about such things as breathing adjust‧ ment, the effect of buoyancy and balance. (See Fig. 1)‧

Breath Holding.—Conditions are entirely different for breathing when one is attempting to learn how to swim, than those found in any other activity.   The face is frequently buried beneath the surface and there is always foam and spray flying about to impede breathing.   No one is ever exactly comfortable in the water until he has learned to hold the breath auto‐ matically when the face is covered with water, and until he has learned how to regulate his breathing to meet these conditions.

In swimming practically all of the breathing is done through the *mouth*.   The inhalation is taken entirely with the mouth and the air is exhaled by the mouth largely and a little through the nose. So to all intents and purposes the beginning swimmer can forget that he has a nose and concentrate wholly on mouth breathing.   The reasons for this will be made clear later on in "Elements of Swimming."

The first thing the non-swimmer masters in this phase of learning is holding the breath.   Standing in waist-deep water and leaning forward the learner inhales through the mouth taking a quick "bite" of air, the face is then laid in the water with eyes and mouth closed and the breath is held for an appreciable length of time before coming up again.   This should be repeated a number of times gradually increasing the length of time the face is under water until the breath can be held for at least ten seconds.   Two things will become apparent to the learner at this stage of learn‐ ing; one, that if the face is laid flat in the water there will be no tendency for the water to enter the nostrils and two, that there will be some difficulty in getting the breath after the head is lifted from the water because of water streaming down the face. If the learner tries to submerge the mouth and nose and still keep the eyes and ears above water, he will find that water will tend to flood the nose because of the angled position of the head. If the entire face is beneath the surface looking down toward the bottom instead of up and forward, the water will stay out of the nostrils. Water streaming down the face does no harm but it may be uncomfortable at first. The best way to get rid of it is to place both hands on the face over the eyes and forehead and wipe downward vigorously, blowing a little through the mouth and nose to clear any loose water. Later this will not be necessary as it is found that water on the face does not hurt the eyes nor impede breathing to any extent.

Rhythmic Breathing.—Following the mastery of breath holding, the learner very quickly proceeds to the next step which is rhythmic breathing. This is nothing more than breathing in series, inhaling through the mouth as the head is rolled to the side and exhaling through mouth and nose as the face is turned downward and buried beneath the surface. The breath is not held and the series is uninterrupted within its duration. While simple in itself, rhythmic breathing is of very great importance in the learning process since adequate ventilation of the lungs at regular intervals is vital to continuous swimming, especially in those styles of swimming in which the face is carried alternately above and below the surface. (See Fig. 2).

It is learned most easily by standing in waist-deep water with the body inclined forward at right angles to the legs. The position of the head approximates that taken in swimming and sequences of breaths can be taken by merely rotating the head from side to face down position and return ten, twenty, thirty, even fifty times without stopping.   It is likewise important that the habit of holding the breath even for a couple of seconds between inhalation and exhalation should not be established as this is one of the chief causes of breathlessness and exhaustion in swimming.   Instead, the rotation of the head should be so controlled that the exhalation beneath the surface can begin just as soon as the inhalation ceases.   Similarly, the exhalation should be so controlled that inhalation can commence as soon as the face emerges from the water.

Undoubtedly, one of the greatest retarding factors in swimming is improper breathing.   Until one has learned to get an adequate supply of air in the cycle of a stroke without breaking that stroke, he will always be limited in endurance and the distance he can cover.   For this reason breathing is introduced early in the process of learning how to swim to be established as a good habit.   It is far too easy to develop faulty habits in swimming to leave anything so important to chance development.

Seeing under Water.—Opening the eyes beneath the water can be tried by the learner at this point in his progression.   It does not hurt and a few trials will convince that one can see quite well under the surface. Outlines are blurred and somewhat indistinct to be sure, but form, action, and even color can be distinguished readily if the water is at all clear.   A few trials will prove that the contact of the water on the eyes is not unpleasant or uncomfortable and, henceforth, the learner will keep the eyes open whenever he is beneath the surface both as a convenience and a matter of safety.

Buoyancy.—The learning swimmer as stated before, becomes sensibly aware of loss of weight almost from his first entry into the water, but has yet to prove to himself that the water will support practically all of his weight. Again it is important for the learner to know whether he can float and how much buoyancy he possesses, before he attempts to swim. It is almost universally believed by beginning swimmers that strokes of arms and legs must be used to bear the body up and keep from sinking. If they do not learn early that the body's natural buoyancy will serve to keep them on the surface, they will for some time attempt to divide their stroking movements, using the larger part of the effort to bear them up and the little remainder to propel themselves through the water. This practice will serve only to bring about quick exhaustion and (more important) cause the head to lift and drop above and below the surface, thus making rhythmic breathing virtually impossible. A safety factor of great value also is found by the beginner in acquiring the ability to float or rest in a floating position on the back. Later on, when the learner has mastered the first rudimentary beginning swimmer strokes, he will find that frequently they may prove to be inadequate and that he may become tired at a time or in a place (deep water) where to stop stroking may mean to endanger his life. If under such circumstances, the beginner has the ability to turn on the back and rest in a floating position, it may conceivably be a factor in saving his life. So, even before actual swimming is begun, the novice should get some idea of how much buoyancy he possesses and master the fundamentals of resting on the back.

The process of learning how to float is started in water of sitting depth.   Here the beginner sits on the bottom up to his chin.   Placing the hands to the rear

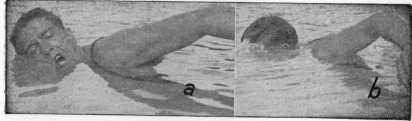

Fig. 2.—Rhythmic breathing.

on the bottom, the head is laid back in the water until all but the face is beneath the surface.   First the legs and then the hips are raised from the bottom until the whole body is supported on the hands.   Gradually the

Fig. 3.—Beginner floating in extreme shallow water.

position is adjusted and the weight becomes water-borne.   Less and less use is made of the hand support and when the balance is caught the hands are slowly withdrawn from the bottom and extended sideward at shoulder level.   In most cases the legs will immediately drop again until the heels are resting on the bottom, nevertheless most of the weight will be sup-

Fig. 4.—Learning how to float in waist deep water.

ported by the water. With repeated attempts the arms may be moved gently (always under water) to an extended position beyond the head, the hips may be dropped slightly and the feet brought up from the bottom until the learner is floating free. (See Fig. 3).

The back floating position should be practiced repeatedly until the learner feels that it is being done with little effort and that he is reasonably comfortable in this position. Gradually he should work away from shore until the floating position is being taken in water waist-deep, starting from a squatting position and returning to it before attempting to stand up. In floating practice, the back should always be toward shore so that if the learner drifts at all it will be toward the shallows rather than outward into deep water. It is always desirable to have a partner or "buddy" standing by to aid in the first few attempts to recover the footing. (See Fig. 4).

In tanks or places where the minimum depth will not permit taking a sitting position on the bottom, the aid of an instructor or partner is necessary. Support is given the learner in first trials by placing one hand under the back of the neck and the other beneath the hips. Gradually the hands are eased away, first from the hips and then from the neck as the learner settles into a comfortable and balanced position.

Prone Floating.—Floating in the face-down position is a parallel worthwhile accomplishment for the beginner to master. While this is not a resting position except within the limits of the learner's breath-holding capacity, since the face is buried in the water, it is the standard position assumed for all styles of swimming in which the swimmer lies on the front. Therefore, the ability to take a comfortable, balanced and relaxed prone position in the water is one of the more vital pre-requirements for actual swimming.

The practice of prone floating is begun in water of

Fig. 5.—Beginner's prone float.

sitting depth.   Lying out-stretched supported only by the hands on the bottom, the beginner takes a full breath, lays the face in the water and gently lifts the hands from the bottom and extends the arms beyond the head.   The whole upper body will be water-borne as it was in the back-floating position, and if the toes rest on the bottom a slight push will raise them toward the surface to a point where the whole body is floating free.   This action should be repeated a number of times until relaxation, ease and some sense of balance are achieved.   (See Fig. 5).

Jelly Fish Float.—In tanks and places where the minimum depth of the water averages waist-deep, a little different procedure is employed to learn prone floating.   Instead of starting with the prone position, the beginner does the "jelly fish" float as a preliminary step in the learning sequence.

Standing in water waist-deep, the beginner bends forward placing the hands on the thighs.   Taking a breath, the face is submerged and slowly the hands are slid down the legs until they reach and clasp the ankles. No effort is made to bend the knees and lift the feet off the bottom. As a rule, even before the ankles are reached, the gradually submerging upper body begins to buoy the beginner up, the feet float free of the bottom and the body is suspended at the surface with the rounded back showing above water. Footing is recovered by slowly lifting the upper body and head toward the surface allowing the feet to settle once more to the bottom. It must be emphasized that this step in learning should be done slowly and no effort should be made to stand erect until the feet are well placed and the body balanced over them. In later trials, the ankles are released and the arms and legs are allowed to hang vertically. (See Fig. 6).

Now comes a step in the learning process of considerable importance. Again the jelly fish floating position is taken and gently the arms are lifted forward and the legs extended backward until the learner is lying in a fully extended prone position. Then, immediately and within the capacity of one breath, the beginner folds up, returns to the jelly fish float position and stands. This is repeated several times or until the beginner can accomplish it without difficulty. If the legs have to be bent and the knees drawn toward the chest in order to get to the feet, it is even better than trying to jackknife back to position with the legs held straight. Two things are accomplished in mastering this phase of learning. First, the beginner learns how to take the extended position used in swimming and second, he learns how to get back on his feet, in water too deep to permit placing the hands on the bottom.

This process of taking the jelly fish floating position, extending to the prone position and returning to the

feet, is also used as the *second* step in deeper water for
those who have learned to float prone in water of
sitting depth.

Fig. 6.—Progressive steps in jelly fish float.

At this point, it is well to check back on what the
beginner may have accomplished, in the development
of the preceding skills. He has learned and (more
important) has practiced over and over again a series
of basic skills upon which he will build through all his
swimming experience. If there was any fear of the
water, it has been largely overcome. Physical and
mental adjustment to the new element has been made
and he is no longer conscious of the lower temperature
of the water or pressure upon the chest. The beginner
has learned how to catch and hold the breath when
the face is submerged, that the eyes may be opened
under water without discomfort and that while one
cannot inhale beneath the surface, no difficulty is
experienced in exhaling there. He has proven to
himself that he possesses some buoyancy and that the

water will support most, if not all of his weight in both the back floating and prone positions. He has taken repeatedly two of the positions he will use in swimming on the back and on the front, and has learned to get to the feet even where he cannot touch bottom with the hands. In all of these skills he has been learning constantly to maintain his balance and to relax, to let the water bear him up, to work with it instead of fighting it. In short, he has made a good beginning toward feeling "At home in the water." Now, and now only, is the beginner ready to learn how to stroke so that he may make progress through the water.

Propulsion

The Prone Glide.—The first propulsive movement through the water employs no stroke. Instead it requires nothing more than a shove of the feet against the bottom and a long slide in the prone position along the surface. (See Fig. 7).

The learner stands in thigh to waist-deep water and bends forward with arms extended beyond the head. The knees are bent, the body is inclined forward and the balance is lost. A quick bite of air is taken, the feet are thrust against the bottom, and in a stretched prone position the learner glides out along the surface a distance of anywhere from two to five body lengths. As momentum ceases, the knees are brought to the chest, the extended arms are pressed down, the head lifted and the beginner stands. The learner should strive in subsequent trials to take off smoothly, stream-line the body, and experience the thrill of slipping through the water in balance and with ease. (See Fig. 8).

The Glide on the Back.—The glide on the back is another useful step in the learning process and should be practiced along with the glide on the front. This is done by slowly submerging to the neck in water waist-

Fig. 7.—The prone glide.

deep, pushing off with the chin tucked well into the throat and the arms at the sides, and sliding a little

way along the surface. The thrust against the bottom
is far less vigorous than it is in the prone glide, to
avoid burying the face in the water. Recovery to
standing position is accomplished by drawing up the

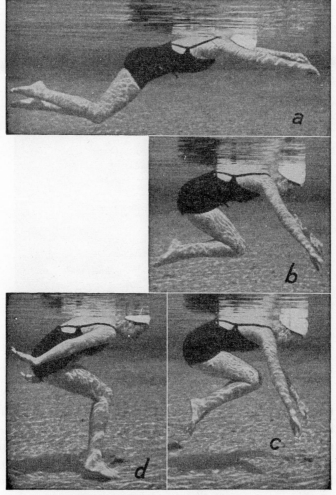

Fig. 8.—Steps in recovering footing.

knees, rounding the back, and lifting the head forward. No attempt should be made to stand until the tucked up body settles to the vertical. (See Figs. 9 and 10).

Fig. 9.—The glide on the back.

The Kick Glide on the Front.—As the beginner practices the glide, he will note that, unless he is quite buoyant, the feet start to settle to the bottom as momentum decreases. Almost automatically this will prompt him to start kicking in an effort to keep the feet at the surface. At this point, the first crude stroking movements are begun.

The leg stroke first to be mastered by the learner is merely a loose easy alternate striking of the water with the shin and the top of the foot in what is known as

Fig. 10.—Recovering footing from back glide.

the beginner's flutter kick. The legs are thrashed up and down with knees bending flexibly and with considerable depth to the stroking movement. Before using this stroke in the kick glide, it is well for the learner to practice it either resting on the hands in shallow water or bracketed against the side or end if in a pool. In practice, the beginner should strive to lift and drop the whole leg from the hip, striking vigorously with the lower leg on the down drive. When the co-ordination is established and enough thrust is developed to tend to force the learner forward, the kick glide may be tried. (See Fig. 11).

In the kick glide, the learner starts as in the straight glide previously mastered but when he gets into gliding position, the legs start their alternate up and down thrash, thus driving him along the surface for distances limited only by the capacity to hold the breath.

The Kick Glide on the Back.—The kick glide on the back is practiced similarly either in shallow water or bracketed against the side.   There is, however, a little variation in the leg stroke.   Instead of trying to beat the water with the lower leg, the legs are pedalled with the sole of the foot pushing down and backward on the down stroke and the front of the foot "spooning" the water up and backward on the upstroke.   In the kick glide on the back, the arms are held at the side and the face remains above the surface at all times. No limit is placed, therefore, on the length of time that this stroke may be sustained except the natural limits of the area and the strength of the learner.   (See Fig. 12).

The kick glide on both the front and the back should be practiced many times until the learner achieves well-balanced position, effective thrust or traction, some endurance and the ability to get off and back on the feet with ease.

The Arm Stroke on the Front.—This stroke for beginners is almost universally known as the "dog-paddle" which, indeed, it resembles somewhat.   Contrary, however, to popular opinion, this stroke is not merely a baby way of paddling through the water. Properly done it contains all the basic elements for effective use of more highly developed arm strokes and when carefully mastered it serves as the fundamental stroke out of which all other arm strokes are developed.   (See Fig. 13).

The stroke may be described as an alternate forward reaching extension of the arms, followed by a pull back under the body to the vertical and a bent arm recovery back to the extended position. When properly co-ordinated, the learner is constantly sliding on one forward extended arm while the other is pulling

Fig. 11.—Kick glide on the front.

back under the body. It may be practiced standing in shallow water with the body bent forward at right angles along the surface or the feet may be supported by a partner or the instructor. When the co-ordination is mastered, practice is continued in the prone gliding position with little or no movement of the legs. Within the limits of one breath, the learner strives to get the "feel" of the stroke in not only its pull but its recovery and extension or reach.

The Arm Stroke on the Back.—It seems to be a perfectly natural thing for a swimmer to use an arm stroke almost automatically, whenever he turns on the back. This stroke is usually nothing more than a series of little pushing or half-sculling movements of the hands, very close to the sides.

The easiest arm stroke for the beginner to use in this position is "finning." To fin, the arms are fully

extended along the sides, hands are then drawn along
the sides a distance of ten to twelve inches.   The finger
tips are extended outward and the hands are pressed

Fig. 12.—Kick glide on the back.

out, around and backward toward the feet returning
to the starting position.   Finning is nothing more than
a series of thrusts with the hands, toward the feet,
which tend to push the swimmer backward through the
water.   (See Fig. 14).

Some learners in practicing and developing this
stroke fall naturally into the habit of circling the hands
outward on the draw and thrusting them back and
downward with a semi-circular scooping motion.   This
is a half-scull and is even more effective for propulsion
than "finning."

The Combined Stroke on the Front.—When the
beginner has learned to use the legs in the up and down
thrash, and the arms in dog-paddle fashion, somewhat
effectively, he is ready to combine the two in his first
co-ordinated stroke or style of swimming.   This is
the beginner's stroke called by Ralph Thomas "the
human stroke."   The stroking movements used, if
assembled or co-ordinated in their right relationship,
will produce a fairly effective means of moving through

the water for short distances. The co-ordinated stroke consists of first, a pull of the right arm and a down beat of the left leg and second, a pull of the left arm and a

Fig. 13.—Arm stroke on the front.

downward beat of the right leg. In breathing, the breath is taken above the surface as one arm is extended and pulled downward, then the air is exhaled below the surface as the same arm is recovered. One breath should be taken and exhaled in every complete cycle of the stroke. (See Fig. 15).

For the beginner to learn how to co-ordinate the stroke, it is simplest to start with a prone glide, then pick up the stroke with the legs, and finally add the arm stroke. No attempt should be made to breathe in the first few trials until the relation of arms and legs is worked out. Within the capacity of one breath, several complete cycles of stroke may be taken without discomfort. When the co-ordination is well established the head may be raised and breathing fitted into the stroke. Continued practice will gradually produce effectiveness in stroking which will permit the learner to carry the mouth and nose above water at all times and do all his breathing, including exhalation over the surface.

For those who are anxious to move on to more

Fig. 14.—Finning.

advanced stroking movements, the so-called modified crawl is the next step. When the "human stroke" is mastered and can be swum with ease, the learner may, if he so desires, begin to recover the arms over the water in a hand-over-hand style of stroking provided he has the strength and flexibility to do so. It must be remembered, however, that this windmill type of two-beat stroke is only a crude example of crawl stroke swimming as different from a true finely-co-ordinated crawl as an inexpensive assembled clock differs from a finely constructed watch.

Combined Stroke on the Back.—Out of the stroking movements learned on the back, the beginning swimmer can make also a combined stroke of some value. To the up and down churning movement of the legs can be added at regular intervals the finning or sculling thrust of the hands.   No arbitrary relationship of arm and leg strokes can be determined in this case, nor is it necessary to fit the breathing accurately

Fig. 15.—Beginner's stroke on front.

into the cycle of the stroke.   Starting with a glide on the back, the learner churns the legs up and down and then fits the arm stroke in at regular intervals.   As this is a resting stroke for beginners no attempt should be made to get much speed from it.   Instead, the stroking should be rather gentle and serve only to maintain a comfortable position on the back with very little motion through the water.

All gliding, stroking, and combined stroking practice up to this point have been done in water of standing depth.   No attempt should have been made heretofore to try out the strokes in deep water.   When the beginner has reached the point where he can swim a full minute continuously along shore or back and forth in a restricted shallow area, using the "human stroke" and when the combined stroke on the back can be employed effectively for a period of at least half a minute, the beginner is just about ready to try out his strokes in deep water. Before he does this, however, two or three safety skills should be mastered. The beginner now has the ability to swim straight away on the front or the back but has not yet learned how to turn back on his course or roll from the front position to the back and vice versa. Furthermore, he has had no experience in getting into swimming position except by pushing off from a standing position on the bottom.

Changing Direction.—Before the learner swims directly outward into deep water he should know how to turn around and come back. The important thing for the beginner to remember in changing direction is that the feet and legs should not be permitted to drop to the vertical so that he will have to struggle to regain swimming position. First turns should be fairly wide with the head turning and the arms reaching in stroke toward the side to which he wishes to turn. With subsequent trials the turn can be gradually shortened until the learner can turn about and come back along his course.

Turning Over.—It serves little purpose for the beginning swimmer to be able to swim both on the front and on the back if he is unable to change from one to the other with ease.

To roll from the front to a position on the back requires nothing more than allowing the feet to drop a little and to make the turn on one extended arm. The head is rotated in the direction in which the beginner wishes to turn; the extended arm supports the weight

while the other arm is drawn across the body and
extended to the opposite side.

The turn from the back to the front position is not

Fig. 16.—Turning from back to front position.

quite so easily accomplished by the beginner but after
a few shallow water trials it is readily mastered.   To
turn from the back to the front, if the learner wishes to
turn to the left, the right leg is crossed over the left, the
right arm is drawn across the chest and the turn is
made.   To turn to the right, naturally the left leg and
arm are brought across to the other side.   (See Fig. 16).

Levelling Off.—One of the commonest difficulties
the beginner faces when he finally progresses to deep
water is that of getting into a horizontal swimming
position from the vertical.   His final practice before
graduating to deep water, therefore, should include
these skills.   (See Fig. 17).

First, taking a position facing the shore in water
chin deep, the beginner leans a little forward and with
a minimum of thrust against the bottom, swims his
way to the horizontal and continues to shore.

Second, under the supervision of instructor or a
swimmer, the beginner swims a few feet out into deep

Fig. 17.—Levelling off from vertical position.

water, turns about and deliberately allows his body to settle to the vertical, then swims his way up to the horizontal again and continues to shallow water.

Third, still under supervision, the beginner leaps feet foremost from low dock or pool side into deep water, comes up, levels off and swims to safety.

The learner is then ready to test the effectiveness of his strokes in deep water by leaping into deep water feet foremost, coming up, levelling off, and swimming on the front for a distance of twenty to twenty-five yards. Then without stopping, to turn about and swim back toward the starting point. Half way along the return course the learner turns on to his back and strokes in that position for at least five yards, then turns again and completes his swim on the front. When this can be done with full confidence the beginner is ready to undertake training in the regular or standard strokes.

A brief review of what has been accomplished will show that the learner has really made progress. The fact that he has learned how to swim a little, while important, is only a part of his accomplishment. In definite phases of development he has learned and mastered certain fundamental skills upon which as a foundation, he can develop as a swimmer. They follow.

The beginner has learned:

1. Where and under what conditions he will be safe.

2. The limitations of his newly acquired strokes.

3. To adjust himself mentally and physically to the water.

4. How to hold the breath when the face is submerged, and how to breathe rhythmically.

5. How to use natural buoyancy for resting, and in swimming.

6. To keep the eyes open under water.

7. To get off and on the feet in shallow water without difficulty.

8. Two positions for floating and swimming. (on the back and on the front)

9. A fundamental leg stroke on both the front and the back.

10. A fundamental arm stroke, front and back.

11. How to swim a combined stroke on the front.

12. How to swim a combined resting stroke on the back.

13. To turn from the front to the back and from the back to the front.

14. To change direction while swimming the "human stroke."

15. To level from a vertical position by swimming up to the horizontal.

16. To enter deep water feet foremost, come to the surface and swim.

17. To navigate to a limited extent in deep water.

If these simple water skills have been thoroughly learned and mastered, they will serve as the fundamental or basic structure upon which real swimming ability will be developed soundly, safely, and progressively. The whole process of learning how to swim by the method given may be accomplished by almost anyone if he follows the progression and does not attempt short cuts. One cannot, however, see himself in action and as he is often unaware of poor position or false motion, he will proceed on a trial and error basis, thus handicapping his progress and slowing down the learning process. Under a competent instructor, who detects mistakes and encourages the learner by suggestion, correction, and criticism, progress will always be smoother and more rapid.

CHAPTER III

ELEMENTS OF SWIMMING

When anyone has gone through the process of learning how to swim and has finally succeeded in propelling himself a distance of several yards in the manner described heretofore, he cannot be called a swimmer any more than a toddling child can be said to be truly walking. As a matter of fact, like the child, he has achieved only uncertain equilibrium in a new position and a crude form of locomotion by means of a series of poorly related movements. In it there is little rhythm and a great expenditure of energy and no matter how assiduously the stroke may be practiced, it can never be developed into a smooth and easy style of swimming suitable for use in a sustained effort. The "human stroke" (dog paddle commonly) at this point has fulfilled its purpose. It has helped to overcome fear, has demonstrated that propulsion in the water is possible and has given the non-swimmer the elementary bases of pull, thrust, co-ordination and breathing. Now, natation as an art, begins and the "human stroke," as a means of water locomotion, is discarded. No longer will the beating movements of the feet be used, except in play. The arms will be employed henceforth, in much more rhythmic and efficient movements. Again, as the child learns from this point to stand in position, walk easily, run, jump and even dance, the beginner will learn to float, swim easily, swim rapidly, tread water and even perform complicated water evolutions if his interest prompts him to pursue it to that end. At the very least, he will want to be able to float, to tread water, and to swim as easily as he walks. Henceforth, every position and movement will be taken or made with studied care to discipline legs and arms and to bring them under control. Carefully controlled movements, first singly and then in pairs, are practiced with an intense concentration that permits but small deviation from correct use. Only after this is accomplished should any attempt be made to co-ordinate the legs and arms in any of the known styles of swimming.

Basic Swimming Motions

The methods by which one may achieve support and locomotion are singularly few in number, the variations of these methods are many. Basically, however, the whole experience of mankind in the water has produced but three ways of floating, three of treading water, three of using the legs and three of the arms in swimming. In addition there are only nine recognized styles of swimming (more generally known as strokes), and five of these are variations of the other four. There are many variations of these positions and movements and numerous combinations and adaptations of them but they are not basic and for the most part are used only in floating and swimming stunts.

The question can be asked at this point "Why should so much emphasis be placed upon swimming expertly when all that is wanted by the vast majority of people is enough knowledge of this art to use the water comfortably and with safety?" The answer to this question was stated simply and adequately nearly a century ago by Clias, a swimming authority of that time. In "A new and complete treatise on the Art of Swimming," published in 1835, he wrote, "We can have but little pleasure and no safety in the water as indifferent swimmers. Experience proves to us that more fatal accidents happen to those who swim imperfectly than those who cannot swim at all, the latter having no temptation to expose themselves to danger." This is held to be just as true today as it was then and should, therefore, be taken as a precept by all who attempt to learn how to swim.

Swimming Fundamentals

Thousands of self-taught swimmers, through lack of understanding of the underlying principles which govern swimming development, go through the whole painful "trial and error" process in learning to swim. Some of these eventually learn how to swim quite well, by close observation and imitation of skilled swimmers and constant practice but the vast majority fumble their way along with crude even though ingenious methods of compensating for their lack of fundamental knowledge. Because of this they must always be limited to short distances or very slow progress through the water and may never know the joy and satisfaction that comes with skilled performance.

The whole evolution of the art of swimming has produced a number of broad fundamental principles that are common to all swimming, which, if properly understood and incorporated in swimming practice, make progression easier but which, if ignored or imperfectly understood, make swimming development uncertain and difficult. Their proper use is the foundation for a degree of expertness limited only by the adaptability and strength of the swimmer. Some of these principles have been alluded to under "Learning How to Swim." Now, however, they must be discussed more fully to serve as a basis for complete understanding of the fundamental principles which govern the progress of the swimmer.

Use of Buoyancy.—It has been stated before that the specific gravity of the average body is something less than that of water. So, if the whole body is immersed the water will exert upward pressure tending to support it at or near the surface. In certain positions on the back or suspended perpendicularly with the head thrown back, this margin of buoyancy is enough to permit the average bather to keep the face above water and breathe comfortably, without motion. In a position on the front or the side, however, too much of the weight of the head has to be carried above the surface in order to breathe, to permit floating motionless. Since the greater part of all swimming is done in these positions, buoyancy cannot be relied upon wholly by the swimmer to maintain him at the surface in a position in which he can get air freely. In these positions (front and side) some momentum is necessary to offset the weight of the head carried above the surface and to supplement the swimmer's natural buoyancy. It should be noted at this point that *momentum* is indicated as the desirable adjunct to buoyancy, not *supporting* movements. (This does not apply, of course, to treading water or swimming in place where movements have of necessity to be supporting.) It is this that almost all novice swimmers fail to understand when they begin to practice strokes, in that they have the tendency to employ the greater part of the stroking movement, especially of the arms, *downward* against the water, in the erroneous belief that it is essential to keeping the head high enough to breathe properly. In so doing, they assume a position somewhat above their normal floating level which demands great expenditure of energy to hold and because of this they tire quickly. All that needs to be remembered really is that one should swim through the water and not try to swim above it. Only in this way can the buoyancy of the individual be employed effectively.

Propulsion.—Water is a fluid and elastic medium. Since it is a fluid it has the property of flowing around a body immersed in it, and gives way before a body moving against it. Contrariwise, as it has some consistency, it may be pressed against for leverage to achieve motion. This is the physical basis of swimming. A person swimming thrusts or presses firmly enough against the water to overcome its resistance and thereby progresses or swims.

Propulsion is effected by using arms and legs in what are known as strokes. A stroke is made up of a pull or thrust of arm or leg, and a recovery. The pull or thrust is the positive portion of the stroke which tends to drive the swimmer through the water; the recovery is negative in that it contributes nothing and actually, in greater or lesser degree, according to the type of stroke used, offers resistance to progress. According to Steedman of Australia (1867) "Strokes made in the line of progress are negative; positive strokes are those made in the opposite direction, and all movements made in any other direction are more or less negative, as they approach or recede from the direction of progress."

Strokes are the movements of the arms and legs made in swimming to propel or, in some positions to support the body, in the water. They are made by pressing backward against the water with the largest possible arm or leg surface to limits consistent with strength, maintenance of equilibrium and recovery in the easiest and least resistant manner possible.

Some stroking movements are almost wholly positive or propelling in action. Examples of this may be found in sculling with the hands and flutter kicking with the legs. Other strokes produce very little negative action in the recovery, notably any arm stroke that is recovered over the surface. Strokes of this character produce speed but are almost continuous in operation allowing very short intervals for muscle groups to rest and recover. These strokes also are made almost wholly in line with the body as it progresses through the water. The crawl strokes are examples of this.

It is not strange that the group of stroking movements which are strongest, the scissors and breast stroke kicks of the legs and the breast stroke pull of the arms, also offer the most pronounced examples of negative action in recovery. The wider the stroke, naturally, the more resistance must be offered to progress in getting arms or legs into position for stroking. On the other hand, the wide strokes afford a much longer resting interval in the glide.

So there are two distinct types of stroking movements, the first of which bases its efficiency upon a minimum of negative action. The second is effective, despite the negative part of its action, because each stroke is followed by a gliding resting interval. Each type has much to recommend it and each has definite uses.

Arm Strokes.—Arm strokes are made with the broad flat surface of the hand and the inner side of the arm and in order that the broadest surface possible may be presented to the water, the fingers are held close together and the thumb is placed firmly against the inner side of the hand, parallel to the first finger. The hand is slightly cupped to prevent "slip." Recovery is made in some arm strokes over water and in others beneath the surface but in all cases the recovery movements are governed by two principles, first, by presenting the smallest possible surface to the resistance of the water and second, by using the least possible muscular effort in getting back to stroking position.

Leg Strokes.—Leg strokes are more variant in action since there are three distinct types employed in swimming. Beating back against the water, as exemplified in the "human stroke" or dog paddle, with the shin and instep is the least effective of the methods used. The application of power is crude and not productive of anything but the poorest of result for the effort expended. Pressing the legs against the water from widely angled positions is stronger than any other form of leg drive despite the handicap of negative action in the recovery portion of the stroke. The scissors and the breast stroke kicks are examples of this. In these strokes a considerable amount of leg and foot surface is driven against the water with corresponding result. The third form of using the legs in swimming is quite unlike any other type of kick. This is the flutter, an alternate undulating action of the legs which when properly done causes the feet to deliver a continuous series of driving thrusts on both the up and down beat with practically no negative action. This stroke, used in the crawl, will be discussed more fully later.

Body Position and Balance.—As everyone knows, the best position for swimming is at or near the horizontal. In this position a minimum of resistance is offered to progress and the weight is more evenly distributed to take advantage of the buoyant effect of the water; that is, in this position there is less likelihood of carrying too much weight above the surface. At the same time legs and arms are low enough in the water to obtain the best possible leverage in stroking.

Observation of swimmers from a point of vantage below the surface, however, indicate that even speed swimmers are much lower in the water than previously had been supposed and in some styles of swimming, notably on the side and in the breast stroke, the body is angled downward toward the feet in the stroke itself, while in the glide, the body rides much more nearly in the horizontal plane.

Apparently two types of body position are in common use among swimmers. The first is the one in which the body is as close to the horizontal position as possible and it is without doubt the more efficient of the two since it produces the best result in propelling force for the amount of energy expended. The second body position is that in which the body is angled downward toward the feet. It is less effective because of the resistance offered to progress but it is more comfortable because the swimmer carries the face above the surface in the stroke either all or a good part of the time. This enables him to breathe much more freely with longer intervals for inhalation but more important, perhaps, obviates the necessity of finely co-ordinating the breathing with the stroke. The author recalls watching a man eighty-one years old swimming in a pond in New England. This old gentleman swam a very slow breast stroke angled downward very sharply which kept his head above the surface at all times. His progress was unbelievably slow yet he swam a mile daily taking approximately two and one-half hours to cover the distance and apparently derived great benefit and enjoyment from it. While any one of the child-swimmers playing about could swim circles around him, few of them could *swim* a mile with the strokes they employed.

Body balance in the water is one of the most difficult of the fundamentals to describe and yet it cannot be ignored for it is of utmost importance to all classifications of swimmers. No one really swims comfortably and with ease until he has found a balanced position for his stroke or strokes. Briefly, a swimmer in balance may be said to have assumed a position which allows freedom of movement in both stroke and recovery, possibility of smooth co-ordination, reasonable comfort in breathing, and advantageous use of buoyancy and body position.

Relaxation.—Relaxation must be discussed and linked up to body position and balance since obviously relaxation is hardly possible if the swimmer's position or balance is faulty.

Muscles held in a state of tension, whether they are making visible effort or not are at work and if the tension is sustained they quickly become fatigued. It is a common fault among swimmers to assume this state of general tension when they enter the water with the result that they soon tire. It may be stated broadly that all groups of voluntary muscles not

directly involved in stroking should be relaxed and
that muscles employed in a stroking movement
should, as soon as the effort is completed, relax at once
so that they may rest. An example or two may be
cited to illustrate the point. Contact with cool water
causes exhilaration which manifests itself by an almost
involuntary contraction of the muscles. In the first
plunge and brief swimming dash, it is the usual thing
for many swimmers to arch the ribs high and pull in
the muscular wall of the abdomen. In so doing they
greatly inhibit breathing and since they are getting an
insufficient supply of oxygen they tire quickly. Or a
swimmer attempting a burst of speed over a relatively
short distance performs his stroking movements so
hurriedly he does not relax even in the recovery portion
of his stroke. As a result he soon "dies off" and
either quits entirely or finishes with a much slower and
less fatiguing stroke.

Breathing.—Faulty breathing is a handicap under
which far too many persons in all classifications of
swimming perform. As stated heretofore, an inadequate supply of oxygen is one of the chief causes of
fatigue and it is more often apt to be breathlessness
which causes a swimmer's difficulty and inability to
continue than it is muscular fatigue. Furthermore,
incorrect breathing all too frequently affects the health
of swimmers, affecting as it does the upper part of the
respiratory tract, particularly the sinuses of the head.
Swimming especially in the newer strokes, requires an
exactness and rhythm in breathing not encountered in
any other form of physical activity, yet it is rarely
dealt with adequately until a swimmer has become
expert enough to enter competition. It is so important, however, both from the standpoint of health as

well as efficiency that correct application of its principles should start as soon as a person begins to learn how to swim.

In many styles of swimming on the front or the side, the face is carried beneath the surface a good part of the time, owing to the necessity for holding the head in line with the spine to get better body position and balance in the stroke. In the cycle of the stroke there is only a brief interval in which the face lifts or turns to come above the surface for air and it is then that the inhalation is taken. Since the interval is so short, air must be taken at a gulp through the mouth as the nostrils are far too small to take in an adequate supply of air before the face is again buried beneath the surface. This fact is well understood and practiced by most swimmers; what is done after the face goes under water is where the major difficulty lies. Usually novices hold the breath while the face is under water and attempt to exhale when the face comes above the surface again, before taking the next breath. If accomplished at all, this has to be done so explosively that an entirely inadequate supply of air is inhaled and after only a few strokes breathlessness develops to such an extent that the swimmer must stop or change his stroke. Furthermore, the very act of holding the breath contributes to breathlessness. Exhalation must take place beneath the surface in the cycle of the stroke unless the swimmer is employing a stroke which permits him to keep the head above water at all times.

This fact has been recognized for years and for a generation at least, learning swimmers have been told "to inhale through the mouth above the water and exhale through the *nose* below the surface." One

serious omission and one grievous error are present
in this admonition. First, rarely has the swimmer
been instructed to begin the exhalation as soon as the
inhalation is completed so that breath holding would
be eliminated, and second, and much more important,
the breath should *not* be exhaled solely through the
nose.

Man drinks through his mouth and breathes through
his nose, although he can and often does use the mouth
for breathing. The mouth being used to water, can
take in air readily and not be irritated if some water
gets in at the same time. The nose, however, is
sensitive to water and if some is taken in with a breath
of air the effect is extremely uncomfortable, causing
gasping, choking, and sneezing which effectually
disrupt the normal process of breathing. Since the
face is so close to the water in swimming, even when
rolled or lifted to clear the surface for air, and since
the water is agitated by the action of the swimmer,
some water in the form of spray is almost bound to be
taken in when the breath is taken. Because of this
it is quite understandable why the mouth and not the
nose should be used to take in air while swimming.
The reason why a swimmer should exhale through the
mouth is a bit obscure and requires further explanation.

To exhale through the nostrils alone in the comparatively brief interval in the cycle of a stroke when
the face is buried beneath the surface, requires a
distinct effort; the air must be pushed out quite
forcibly. If there is any water in the throat and there
generally is, the act of forcibly exhaling the air through
the nose would carry this water in droplets or finely
divided spray along with it. If this water was merely
pushed out through the nasal passages no ill effect

other than irritation would be manifest but, unfortunately, there are other places within the head into which this moisture may be blown. There is no single guiding tube which will insure that loose water will be discharged through the nostrils. Forcible pressure is quite likely to distribute it, driving it from the nasopharynx into the tubes leading to the ears and even into the sinuses of the head. Aside from the irritation caused by water entering where water has no place unless it is absolutely sterile, infectious organisms or germs may be carried with it. Even sterile water will no longer be sterile after it has washed the mucous membranes of the mouth and throat.

If the exhalation is made with the mouth open, less pressure will be needed to force the air out and it will take less time. While most of the air will escape through the mouth, some will inevitably trickle out through the nostrils but the pressure will not be great enough to force droplets into places where they may cause trouble.

It is most distressing to those who know what the consequences may be, to note how commonly accepted as inevitable, a "head full" of water is among swimmers. The beginning swimmer emerging from an involuntary plunge beneath the surface spouting a stream of water from the nostrils, is not only uncomfortable but in danger of developing serious infection. The swimmer hopping on one foot and vainly thumping the side of his head in an effort to get water out of his ear, water which may have been driven into the middle ear from the inside, offers another example of what faulty breathing may do. And finally, the accomplished swimmer bending over in the locker room to tie a shoe an hour after he has emerged from the water, observes without distress a thin stream of water dripping from his nose. He may not be distressed but he might be if he knew that it was draining from his sinuses.

These things have too often branded swimming, especially in pools, as dangerous to health, when it has been the bad practice and not the water that was at fault. No water need penetrate to the sinuses or to the middle ear, if the bather knows how to hold the breath when submerged or to breathe properly in swimming.

Co-ordination.—When strokes are made at random by the arms and legs, no matter how accurately they are pulled and recovered, they cannot be effective for any length of time. When, however, they are so combined that one or both of the legs or arms are resting or recovering while the others are propelling, and when one part is in position ready to take up the stroke as another part completes its portion, the stroke becomes a continuous propulsive movement. The un-co-ordinated stroke is characterized by jerky, uneven progress which soon tires the swimmer because legs and arms are not getting proper resting intervals.

Likewise, breathing is co-ordinated with the strokes employed. In a stroke it is almost invariably the rule that the swimmer inhales at the point in the stroke where the head is highest, generally as the forward arm (or arms) starts to pull. In some strokes the head is lifted and in others rotated on the neck to bring the mouth above the surface. The face settles or rolls beneath the surface again with the recovery of the arm, or arms, and there the exhalation takes place through the remainder of the stroke and glide.

Glide.—One other thing must be discussed as a fundamental principle of swimming. This, for lack of a better term, may be called the glide. This is the distance between strokes which a swimmer rides, drifts, or slides without visible effort, which may be done with one or both arms extended forward of the head. The most notable examples of maximum glide are found in the breast and side strokes where the long gliding interval between strokes is very definite. At the other extreme, the stroke in which there seems to be little if any glide, is the sprinting crawl stroke. The slower the stroke, the longer the glide. Its value is undoubted as it is progress with little effort and fewer strokes have to be taken to cover a specified distance. It is frequently said of a swimmer in training that he is losing speed because he is "shortening his stroke" when, as a matter of fact, he is losing speed because he is not riding the forward arm or arms.

There are other factors which may be said to be fundamental in swimming such as strength, flexibility, and vital capacity, but they are really secondary and are important not in the initial development of swimming ability but rather in developing stamina and speed. Strength is developed through swimming, as are flexibility and lung capacity. This development may be hastened, however, by special exercises on land designed for the purpose.

Floating

A pleasant sensation it must have been to the first man who, either by accident or design, turned upon his back, ceased moving arms and legs and found to his surprise that his face not only did not sink beneath

the surface but that he could rest and breathe freely
in that position. How suddenly must he have sensed
its value as a safety measure to employ when exhausted
and how quickly it must have been imitated by his
fellows. Of the origin of motionless floating we may
only conjecture but that it is of great antiquity is
undeniable, since it is mentioned in some of the
earliest references to swimming although the terms
"floating" and "swimming" were often used inter-
changeably. Its value, too, is unquestioned because
it may be used by tired swimmers to rest from their
efforts when no artificial support is at hand. Many
persons who have found themselves in the open water
far from land, either by having a boat sink beneath
them or being borne away from shore by currents owe
their lives to their ability alternately to swim and
float until they eventually reached land or until picked
up by rescuers. In an orderly learning progression in
natation, floating is placed first because it is the simplest to execute of all forms of support with or without
propulsion in the water and because it is a factor which
is fundamental to water safety.

As stated before in the beginning of this chapter,
basically, there are only three types of motionless
floating; first, the horizontal, second, the balanced
floating position, and third, the suspended or perpendicular float. The first method is, as the name
implies, a motionless position in the water parallel to
the surface with the greater portion of the body
submerged. In the second type, balanced floating,
the body tends toward the vertical, balancing over the
chest, and only the face and occasionally some portion
of the chest is above water. In the third type, as the
name implies, the body is vertical in the water with

the head thrown back and only the face above the surface.

Classification of Floaters.—In learning to float

Fig. 18.—The buoyancy test.

motionless, all persons fall into one of four groups, according to their body structure. In the first group are those who float at or near the horizontal position without effort. This includes practically all women, most stout people and a few slender persons of both sexes. The second classification is made up of those who tend toward an upright position in floating. This group is composed of practically all men and many slender or athletic women, who lack buoyancy in the legs. In the third class (a small one), are those who have positive buoyancy enough to keep the face above water only when the lungs are inflated to capacity. Finally there is a very small number of persons who because of heavy bones, lean muscles, small lung capacity or any combination of these, have no positive buoyancy and so are unable to float motionless.

Buoyancy Test.—In learning to float one should

Fig. 19.—The horizontal float.

determine whether he is a "floater" or a "sinker" and for this purpose a simple test has been devised. In water breast-deep, the novice slowly submerges to the chin, inflates the lungs to capacity, gently submerges the face as he draws his knees up to his chest and wraps his arms about the lower legs. In this tucked-up position, if any part of the head or back remains above the surface he is a "floater," but if he disappears beneath the surface under these conditions, he is a "sinker" and will be quite unable to stay at the surface without motion. (See Fig. 18).

Horizontal Floating.—For those who have abundant buoyancy well distributed the problem of learning to float is a very simple one. The horizontal position on the back is assumed on the surface, the muscles are relaxed and the hips lowered slightly. In the early trials there may be some tendency to roll over, espe-cially among those who are excessively buoyant.

This may be controlled by extending the arms sideward with the palms turned up and, if necessary, by separating the feet. When this tendency to roll has been counteracted by adjusting the body position, the feet may be brought together and the arms placed in almost any comfortable position in the water. They may be extended beyond the head, clasped behind the neck, held at the sides or even folded on the breast. These fortunate persons are true "floaters" and they may most completely enjoy the emancipation and relaxation that come with this effortless achievement.

Balanced Floating.—The vast majority of men and many women, novices and swimmers alike, believe that they are unable to float motionless. Most of them have tried it at some time or another in their bathing experience. Carefully they have assumed a horizontal position and ceased moving arms and legs, only to note that the legs immediately start to sink and if they persisted in holding the position, to find to their dismay when they reached the vertical that the momentum of the down swing of the legs caused the head to disappear beneath the surface. With envy they watched the stout person or the light-boned slender individual bobbing merrily about with face, breast and toes out of the water and decided they would never be able to float as he does, and gave up trying. In this they were quite right, they would never be able to float as he does, because they had not his well distributed buoyancy; but that the majority of this group have some buoyancy is undeniable, therefore, there must be a method whereby they can learn to float reasonably well. That there is and has been such a method for hundreds of years may be surprising information to many persons but it is a fact that it has been known and taught for a long time as perpendicular floating although this is a misnomer and does not truly describe the method. Since there

Fig. 20.—The balanced floating position.

seems to be no adequately descriptive name in common use for this, the term "balanced" floating is used.

Balanced floating is accurately descriptive of the technique which must be employed by this majority group. A person of the physique now being discussed has only one portion of the body that will float, that part which contains the lungs. Above this part is carried a short heavy bony structure, the head. Below there is the lower part of the trunk, and the legs weighted by heavy bones and masses of lean compact muscle. This portion is, of course, much longer. If this type of person is to float successfully he must contrive to balance himself over his one point of

Fig. 21.—Horizontal float with feet drawn up.

support, the chest. Assuming a vertical position, the head is laid back gently until all but the face is completely immersed, the back is arched in its upper part and gradually all movement is stopped. The arms are gently extended sideward under water with the palms of the hands turned upward. If the balance is true, the person may then rest in a motionless floating position. If there is a good margin of buoyancy the legs may swing forward and upward a little and if in this case the arms are gently extended beneath the surface to a point well back of the head, the floater may achieve an almost horizontal position with consequent greater ease and comfort. In some cases, where the person has extremely heavy lower legs, the balance may be caught by separating the knees and drawing the feet toward the body as the arms are extended to full stretch beyond the head. In this manner, the lever is shortened on one side and lengthened on the other, thereby achieving a better counter-balance.

For swimmers possessed of very little positive

Fig. 22.---Vertical float.

buoyancy, motionless floating is possible only in the vertical position and then only in relatively calm water. The body is brought to the vertical and the head tilted backward until the face is almost at right angles to the body. Gently the arms are extended sideward beneath the surface and movement ceases. The swimmer then hangs suspended by the chin with only the mouth, nose, and eyes showing above water.

A small number of persons who try to learn how to float by the method just described find that it works just so long as the breath is held. When the breath is exhaled, the small margin of buoyancy is lost and the head goes under water. To maintain the face at the surface it is necessary to change the manner of breathing to a gasping exchange of air. That is, the breath must be released explosively and caught again immediately so that the buoyancy is lost but for the moment. Persons who float in this way will never enjoy it and cannot be thoroughly comfortable. Nevertheless, they should master it for use in emergencies.

Non-floaters.—For those who simply cannot float, because of their physical structure, little can be done. They should learn to assume a floating position and maintain it by gentle paddling and sculling movements of the feet and hands. A very slight effort will suffice to keep the face above water and enable such persons to rest.

If the technique of floating is put into a formula which covers all physical types but the last named, it is *buoyancy plus relaxation plus balance plus breath control equals motionless floating*. Some positive buoyancy is necessary, of course. Relaxation is a vital requirement for rest and recovery of tired muscles. Balance is important in all classifications of floating. Breath control is most important for those who have only a small margin of buoyancy.

Motionless floating, if it is to fulfill its purpose of enabling a swimmer to rest in deep water, should be accomplished with reasonable ease. If a swimmer has so little positive buoyancy that, even in the correct position, it is done with difficulty, thereby causing strain and discomfort, its real purpose is defeated. Under such conditions, the position may be taken and the small margin of natural support supplemented by gentle movements of the hands and feet. Such movements may be discontinued altogether in salt water where, because of the increased density of the water, anyone but the rare individual possessed of great specific gravity can float motionless.

Resting in Floating Position.—If it is found that it is not easy to maintain a back horizontal position at the surface, inevitably the bather will employ small arm and leg movements to stay up. If these movements are spasmodic and made at random, they will alternately lift and drop the head above and below the surface until the person is forced to change position in order that he may catch his breath. These movements if employed correctly, however, are simple and can maintain the body in a horizontal position with small effort. Learning them, quite naturally, is the next step in this progression.

Most often it is the drag of the legs which upsets the equilibrium in this position so a simple leg stroke has been devised to support them. An alternate up and down paddling movement of the feet and lower legs is employed. The legs alternately are extended with the toes pointed and the sole of the foot pressed downward gently against the water to a depth of eight to twelve inches. The knee is then bent and the foot is drawn slightly toward the body and immediately extended again. This is the simplest co-ordinated swimming movement to learn because it is very much like walking with very narrow steps. When done correctly the horizontal position may be held easily and if the effort is increased it will drive the body slowly backward.

Sculling

The first paired movement learned was finning.

The second paired movement of the arms known as sculling, may be used for support and propulsion not only in the horizontal position but in almost any attitude in which the body is placed. Its uses are so many and of such variety that it may be stated that it is fundamental to "at homeness" in the water. When skill in its use is acquired and it is incorporated into the bather's equipment of "strokes," its usefulness in supporting the body at the surface, in changing positions and attitudes in the water and for propelling the swimmer easily in almost any direction may be readily demonstrated.

So many swimmers have discovered and developed for themselves this method of using the hands that it can only be assumed that its history is almost as old as the history of swimming itself. Yet, so far as can be learned, no writer saw fit to describe the manner of doing it until 1846 and it was not named until 1876, although some writers had mentioned sculling movements prior to this. Perhaps it was considered to be of insufficient importance or as a trick by earlier writers, hence not warranting accurate analysis or description. However, since its importance as a fundamental to water safety is now well known and since there is some confusion concerning the use of the hands and arms in accomplishing the movement, it merits not only an accurate description but a learning method as well.

First, it should be stated that correct sculling is entirely a hand movement and that the arm is not used except as it rotates in its socket at the shoulder to change the position of the hand and thus facilitate its use, and secondly, that there are no negative recovery movements. Apropos of this, Ralph Thomas writes of sculling "the marvel of proper sculling is that there is no unprofitable action, no slip" . . . and, facetiously, it is suspected, " . . . it must therefore be with this stroke nature intended human beings to swim."

To describe correctly the sculling movement of the hand is not easy. If everyone knew how to scull a boat with an oar it would be stated simply that the arm is used in much the same manner as the oar, but since so few persons know how to use an oar for sculling it must be otherwise described. With a flexing wrist the hand is made to describe a figure of eight in the water, first pressing outward with the little finger angled toward the surface and then with a rotation of the arm inward toward the body with the thumb inclined upward. In its greatest scope it should not exceed twelve inches.

In mastering this stroke it is recommended that the novice sit on the bottom or, in a pool, crouch until all but the head is submerged. The arms are then extended forward about six inches below the surface. From this position the elbows are bent and the hands drawn toward the body about six or eight inches. Then the palms are turned back and outward (thumbs down), and pushed vigorously against the water with a full extension of the arm. At that point the hands are rotated until the little finger is down as the hands are drawn toward the body again. This is followed by a backward and inward push. These movements are being done effectively if they tend to push the person over backward at each thrust of the hands. When the movements are well controlled they should be practiced in sequence at first slowly, then with increasing rapidity, gradually reducing the bend at the elbow, until the movements are made with the hands alone. At this point the body is eased into the back floating position with the chin tucked well into the throat and, employing this stroke close to the sides it will be found that easy progress can be made. This is the best position in which to practice and refine the sculling stroke. Later, other body positions may be assumed and by varying the angle of the fingers and the evenness of the stroke, it may be used for support alone or for propulsion in any direction.

Methods of Using Arms and Legs in Swimming

The various recognized styles of swimming by which it is possible to move easily and comfortably in the water are made up of co-ordinated movements of the arms and legs. These movements vary in direction and in relation to each other according to the style employed. Thus the limbs in some styles of swimming make paired movements in which two arms or two legs make identical motions simultaneously. In others the arms or legs may make identical movements alternately, and in at least one style of swimming identical motions of the arms or the legs may be made independently. These strokes must be practiced singly and then in pairs before any attempt is made to operate both arms and legs in any style of swimming. Of course it would be quite impossible to practice the movements of a single arm or leg in deep water with any degree of comfort or safety but any or all of them may be practiced on land or in shallow water. In fact, the pathway of learning, in this case, should start on land, proceed to the shallows and finally move on to deep water. On land, arm movements may be practiced standing, leg movements mastered while sitting or lying at full length. Leg movements may be practiced in shallow water by lying stretched out supported by the hands placed on the bottom. In a pool where it is impractical to use the bottom for support because of lack of suitable shallow water, the same practice can be had by grasping the edge or the gutter and planing the body out to a horizontal position. Arm movements may be practiced in water breast deep while standing on the bottom. In like manner, artificial floating devices may be used to support the arms while the leg strokes are being practiced and vice versa. The best support for leg stroke practice is the kick board, a piece of plank two or three feet in length and a foot or more in width on which the arms are laid. Water polo and beach balls, cork floats and wings may also be used for this purpose. For supporting the legs while arm strokes are practiced, the rubber tube into which the feet can be inserted is perhaps the best artificial aid although water wings also may be used effectively. These floating supports are much more useful in the later stages of stroke development after the action of the legs or arms has been mastered, and are used to develop strength in the stroke and to measure progress.

If all the foregoing description of the learning method is reduced to its simplest terms these principles must be emphasized. First, the movement of a single arm or leg is mastered with particular attention to the correctness of its action. Second, use of the legs and arms in pairs is mastered, both in simultaneous and alternate stroking. Third, these strokes are repeated over and over again on land and in shallow water at first slowly and then rhythmically until the action is no longer studied but semi-automatic. Lastly, the stroke is refined and strengthened by continued practice with the aid of floating supports. It is almost unnecessary to state that progress in this learning process is much easier and more rapid if governed by the coaching of an experienced swimming instructor.

Leg Strokes.—It is generally known that progress in the water is most efficiently made by using both arms and both legs but observation of self-taught swimmers would lead one to believe that most of them had never heard that the legs are of equal importance with the arms. As a matter of fact it is very easy for the average person to learn to stay afloat and propel himself crudely for a short distance with arm strokes largely and leg movements only incidentally. This may be because arm strokes are more easily and naturally mastered than those of the legs due to greater flexibility and range of movement of the arms and closer proximity to the eyes. In other words, a beginner can see what the arms are doing in swimming but can only sense the action of the legs. Whatever the cause may be, however, it is known that novices who concentrate on arm strokes learn to propel themselves quickly enough but thereafter are always limited in endurance and comfort until the legs are brought under control and made to do their real share. It would seem, therefore, in an orderly learning process that the more difficult portion of the various styles of

Fig. 23.—Progressive movements in the scissors kick.

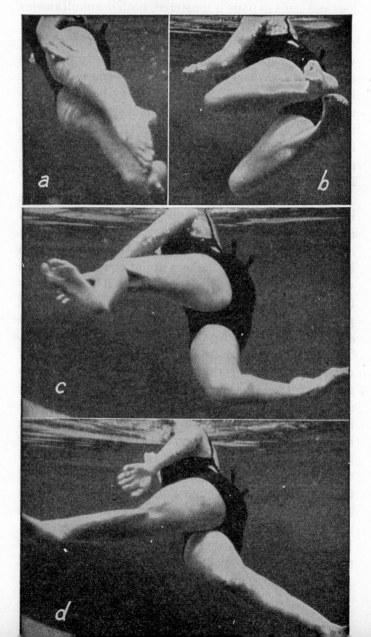

swimming should be mastered primarily. Therefore in this progression the use of the legs is placed before the arms.

It may be stated that there are only two fundamental ways in which the legs may be employed in swimming. They may press the water backward, or they may lash it. Some styles of swimming use one, some another, and still others a combination of two. Other than the "human stroke," no style of swimming uses a press of the legs alone but it is used as a part of the breast stroke and the scissors kick. The lash of the legs belongs only in the crawl strokes, front and back and in the trudgen crawl. The term "kick" although almost universally used to describe leg strokes, is a misnomer as there is not a true kicking movement in any of the strokes employed in swimming.

The Scissors.—Because there is such a difference of opinion among swimming authorities as to which leg stroke is easiest to master, the scissors movement is arbitrarily selected for first consideration and description as the easiest to master. This contention is predicated upon the following facts: The scissors more nearly resembles walking and running movements with which learners are already familiar; it employs muscle groups already smoothly co-ordinated and well-developed by the above means; it is a paired stroke in which the legs make the same kind of motions, simultaneously. (See Fig. 23).

In a position squarely on the side at all times, the legs are held fully extended and closed with the toes pointed. This is the beginning and the finishing position for each stroke of the legs and it must be returned to at the completion of each stroke before the next one is begun. To begin the stroke, the feet are drawn gently toward the body. As the knees are bent, the legs still press close together. As this movement is purely negative it should be made as much in line with the body as possible to decrease resistance. At the point of greatest bend and as a continuation of the drawing movement the legs are separated, the top one moving forward with the knee still bent until the foot is about eighteen inches from the median line of progress. The bottom leg glides gently backward a like distance with the knee considerably bent. Then with a vigorous movement the legs are pressed back against the water and brought together sharply until they meet fully extended in position to begin another stroke. The legs rotate slightly in the stroke, describing a long narrow ellipse. The whole movement is a rhythmic contraction, expansion and extension of the legs in which each movement flows without break or accent into the next one. It begins and continues gently through that portion of it which is negative but as it becomes positive, that is, propelling in its action, muscular power is applied with full vigor in the press until the legs are once more fully extended and together.

No two persons will do this stroke in quite the same manner but no matter what the variation may be, unless it is quite incorrect the principles governing its use will be the same. Some swimmers will wish to make speed and in the very act of speeding up the stroke, will shorten the contraction and narrow the spread of the legs. The range of the stroke will be governed largely by the use to which it is put.

The learning method is relatively simple. First, on land, lying on the side, either on a low stool or box or on the side of the pool with the legs projecting over the water, the paired movements are made and care-fully observed for correctness of position and range. Slowly, at first, with frequent stops to check up, strokes are made in series.   It is inadvisable to use counts to govern these movements.   To use one, two, three, or one, two, three, four tends to develop a jerky action. Rather, descriptive words should be used.   For exam-ple, in the first stages of the learning process to say "I must draw and then separate and press as I extend," will give a fluid rhythm to the stroke even as it is described.   Later when the pattern of the stroke is firmly established in the mind, the action may be speeded up and the governing cadence limited to the phrase "draw and press."   Then the stroke is taken into shallow water for practice, lying on the bottom if it is a beach, bracketed against the side if it is a pool, to adjust the stroke to a denser medium.   Finally it is practiced with a free floating support to learn to balance the body on the side and to make progress.

It will be noted that nothing has been said in this description of the scissors stroke about "squeezing" the legs together to drive the swimmer through the water.   Much was made of the wedging action of the legs in both this and the breast stroke kick in former years without much proof that it was the squeeze that produced propulsion.   In swimming on the side, it is quite apparent that in the major portion of the scissors kick, the legs do not operate in the same lateral plane at all and close observation of the stroke as viewed from beneath the surface, now seems to indicate that the major part of the thrust comes in the press-ing extension of the legs, and that in bringing them together at the completion of the stroke, such addi-tional propelling force as may be developed is the

Fig. 24.—Progressive steps in the flutter kick.

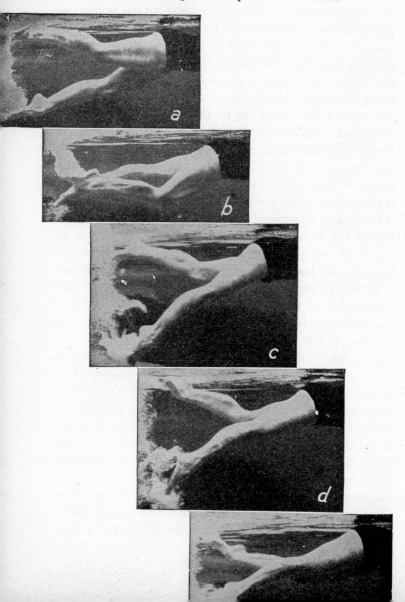

result of straightening the legs and is still a partial thrust backward against the water. Apparently the scissors kick is just an ingenious way of angling the legs outward and then straightening them to exert a maximum of pressure against the water with at least one thigh, the calf of one leg, and the shin of the other; and the sole of one and the instep of the other foot. The closing of the legs together is apparently little more than streamlining while the glide is taken.

The Flutter Kick.—If ever a stroking movement was misnamed it was this one. The word flutter is defined by Webster as "moving with quick vibrations" or "to move agitatedly with little result." This is precisely what hundreds and thousands of learning swimmers do when they attempt to swim the crawl; they vibrate the legs with little result. Understanding of this method seems to have begun and ended with most learning swimmers with the idea that if the legs are alternately shaken up and down in the water that is all there is to it. There seems to be no general understanding among swimmers of the principles involved in the stroke and of its correct execution.

The alternate up-and-down vertical thrash of the legs as exemplified in the "human stroke" has been known apparently for thousands of years. Some primitive peoples in various sections of the world have used it in combination with the hand-over-hand stroke of the arms for unnumbered generations. In comparatively modern times, the stroke was borrowed from the natives of Ceylon and taken to Australia. There it was adopted by the leading competitive swimmers of the time and refined into what has become known as the Australian crawl, the refinement consisting of the development of a synchronized rather than a haphazard method of stroking. This synchronization or timing consisted of using a pull of an arm on one side and a vertical downward thrust of the

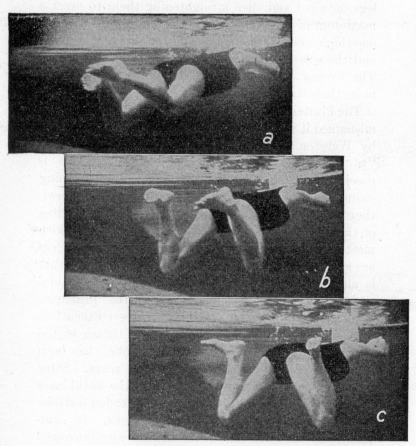

shin and instep of the leg on the other side. This was followed by a pull of the other arm and a kick of the other leg to complete the cycle of the stroke. In this form it was brought to England and the United States by the Cavill brothers, noted swimmers of that time, who used it with remarkable success in racing at sprint distances. It was quickly adopted by speed swimmers in both Europe and America, but from this point on,

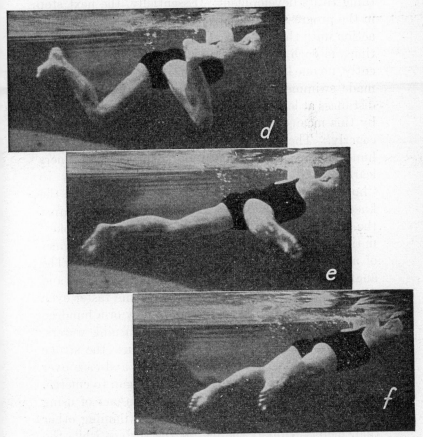

Fig. 25.—Progressive action of the breast stroke kick.

the record of its further development is obscured for a while.

The Cavills themselves, Sundstrom and Daniels, both American swimmers, and others are variously credited with taking the next step in the evolution of what is now described as the American crawl. Actually, it is probable that all of these contributed something to its development. Essentially, the next step in the progression was merely a speeding up of the leg action until they were beating four, six, and even eight times in each cycle of the arms. For a time, apparently, no one knew exactly why the speeded up "kick" made swimmers go faster. The fact that for sprint distances at least, swimmers could improve their times by this means was enough to cause them to adopt it eagerly. The water was thrashed violently in a hundred pools and confusion reigned. Swimmers learning the new stroke were advised variously to "hold the legs rigid from hip to toe" or to "loosen the knee and smash the shin and instep downward against the water." They were told to "narrow the stroke" until it was merely a vibration of the legs; one swimmer of note at least developed a twelve beat crawl. The angle of the legs from the hips was changed again and again. Sprint swimmers swam faster and faster even if they were "all out" at the end of fifty or a hundred yards. Then, out of the welter of churning waters, began to appear swimmers who could use the stroke more slowly and with surpassing grace and ease over ever increasing distances, and reason began to emerge. Perhaps there was something in this manner of using the legs that could do something in swimming other than merely support the feet at the surface while the arms tore through the water in the hand-over-hand stroke. Legs were dropped somewhat lower in the water; emphasis began to be placed on the upward lift of the foot as well as on its downward drive and gradually flexible undulation of hip, knee and ankle began to supplant the vigorous smashing beat of the legs. The number of kicks began to drop back and became stabilized at six and for some conditions at four. Crawl swimming became more and more effective over ever increasing distances and training methods were evolved to help meet the new demands for more strength, flexibility and increased efficiency.

Description of the Stroke.—It has been said of the flutter kick that the swimmers who use it most successfully have "rubber" legs. This may be interpreted as meaning that they have a controlled flexibility of the ankle, knee and hip joints which permits an undulating movement to start at the hip and move progressively to the thigh, to the lower leg and to the foot, where it is finished by a straightening of the leg and a backward and upward lash of the foot. The legs alternately whip up and down in the vertical plane, the upward movement finishing as the heel breaks the surface and the downward stroke pressing to a depth of anywhere from twelve to eighteen inches. These limits are placed on the stroke for greater effectiveness, since any stroking above the surface is wasted effort and any below a depth of eighteen inches increases resistance by throwing the body too far out of the horizontal plane. (See Fig. 24).

Learning Method.—Although there is nothing natural about the flutter kick, its essentials are rather easily mastered if a progressive learning method is followed.

It is doubtful if land drill in the reclining position is of much value in the learning process since in the strained position necessarily assumed the movements of the legs are stiff and awkward. It is better to start the learning process in shallow water either with the hands on the bottom or bracketed against the side of a pool or dock.   In the horizontal position the legs are extended to the rear and close together just below the surface.   The back is flattened and the feet are slightly lower than the hips.   When an easy and comfortable position is assumed, the legs are lifted and dropped alternately.   At first the movements are made slowly as they are brought under control.   The emphasis is placed on the upward lift of the leg.   In the early stages of this process the movements of the feet may be likened to those used in pedalling a bicycle of very low gear, the backward and upward extension of the foot being almost identical in both cases.   After the movements are brought under control they are performed in rhythmic sequence until the actions become semi-automatic.   To establish a rhythm that can be incorporated easily into the whole stroke, it is recommended that the beats or strokes be made in a continuous series of cycles of six with the first and fourth beat of each cycle deliberately accented.   Thus the governing count would be ONE, two, three, FOUR, five, six, or better, LEFT, right, left, RIGHT, left, right, in which a beginning, a mid-point, and an end of each cycle is indicated.

In the second step in the development of this stroke a free floating support is used for hands and arms while strength, endurance and "finish" are developed by continuous rhythmic practice.   Over a defined course the learner slowly "kicks" his way back and forth until the stroke is done smoothly and easily and he is capable of continuing it for a period of several minutes. If the learner is unable to sustain the effort it may be due to one of two things, either he is holding the legs too stiffly or he is stroking too rapidly.   If he makes no perceptible progress the stroke is being done incor-

rectly. Success in the use of this stroke is dependent
upon controlled flexibility and relaxation.

Breast Stroke Kick.—The third method of using
the legs employs probably the least natural movements of any in human swimming. The breast stroke
kick has a stroking motion which uses certain muscle
groups in a manner for which there is no counterpart
in land locomotion. Its history, however, is as old
as that of swimming itself among the many peoples
in the North Temperate Zone and despite its artificial
nature it is surprisingly efficient for some purposes.

Description of Stroke.—Because there is no natural
example which can be cited to illustrate this stroke
and because it combines in a lashing movement two
distinct ways of pressing against the water, it is not
easy to describe. However, its description is possible
by analysis of individual movements of the parts. In
a front horizontal position, the legs are fully extended
and together with toes pointed six to eight inches below
the surface. To begin the stroke the feet are drawn
toward the body as the knees are extended sideward
until the point of maximum bend is almost reached.
At this point, the knees are rotated inward as the
feet and lower legs are slued until they are extended
sideward. Immediately, as a continuation of this
rotating movement, the inside of the lower leg and the
extended foot is pressed back and outward as the
legs are straightened and extended outward at an angle
of 45° or beyond. Then, as a continuation of the
preceding movement, the extended legs are brought
together until they resume the starting position. This
stroke can be done by drawing, extending and squeezing the legs, eliminating the rotation of the knee and
lower leg but it then becomes a series of two negative

and one positive movement, whereas, with the rotation of the knee inward after the draw, immediately followed by a pressing extension and a close, only one negative and one continuous positive movement is made. When this stroke is brought under control and the movements of the legs become a smooth and continuous action, the draw of the feet and rotation of the knees is but one short negative action followed by one complete positive action made up of the pressing extension and the closing of the legs. (See Fig. 25).

Learning Method.—The learning method is begun on land. First, in an erect position, the learner stands on one foot, as the stroke of the other leg is studied, practiced and brought under control. The process is then repeated with the other leg. Then, in a half-reclining position on the ground or the edge of the pool the legs are extended to the front horizontally and the movements of both legs simultaneously are practiced in the face-up position. Thence the stroke is taken into shallow water as described heretofore, either in the prone or face-up position and, finally, the free floating support (kick board), is used to develop strength and rhythm. (See Fig. 26).

Arm Strokes.—The arms serve two purposes in swimming: primarily they are used for propulsion and, secondarily, in all strokes in which they are extended beyond the head they help to support the upper body and maintain equilibrium. It should be noted that they serve to support the body mostly in the extended gliding position and to very little extent in the propelling portion of the stroke.

In recognized styles of swimming there are but three basic methods of using the arms. Each method is composed of a catch, a pull, and a recovery movement which returns the arm to starting position. Of these three basic strokes only one has a name that truly describes the movement and that is the hand-over-

Fig. 26.—Leg stroke practice using kick board.

hand stroke. The other two are related to the two strokes in which they are particularly used and are commonly called the breast stroke and the side stroke pull of the arms. It is difficult to determine in what order these basic arm strokes should be learned since they are only remotely related to each other and ease of mastery is dependent largely upon the individual. To be consistent, however, the preceding progression in the development of leg strokes and in preparation for the co-ordination of the two, the development of the side stroke of the arms is placed first, followed by the hand-over-hand and lastly the breast stroke.

Use of Arms in the Side Stroke.—In a position squarely on the side, the under arm is held fully extended palm turned down beyond the head and in line with the body. The hand catches the water at a point just below the surface and is pulled with the elbow slightly bent, down and somewhat in front of the body to the vertical. As it passes the vertical

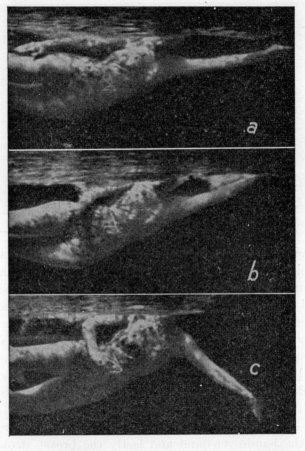

it bends at the elbow and the hand, thumb up, is gently sliced up through the water to a palm-up position just below the neck as the elbow tucks in close to the lower side. At this point, the hand is rotated to a

palm downward position as the arm is fully extended
to its original position. The top arm starts fully
extended along the side. From this point the hand is

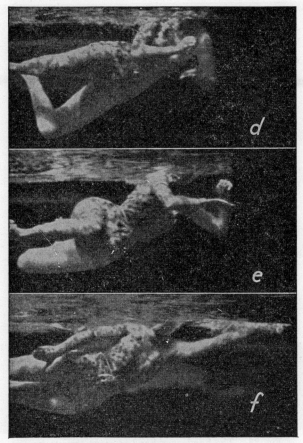

Fig. 27.—Arm action in side stroke.

drawn along the side and as it passes the elbow it is
extended finger-tips foremost and palm down to a
position just under the chin. At this point the water

is caught and the arm is pulled down and backward close to the body until the starting position is reached again.

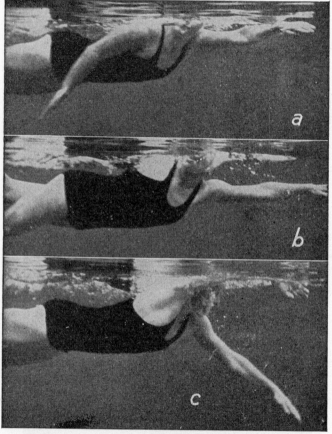

Fig. 28.—The hand-over-hand or crawl arm stroke.

To synchronize the two motions into one continuous propulsive effort is not difficult. From the starting position, as the under arm is pulled downward in stroke, the top arm is moved forward to stroking posi-

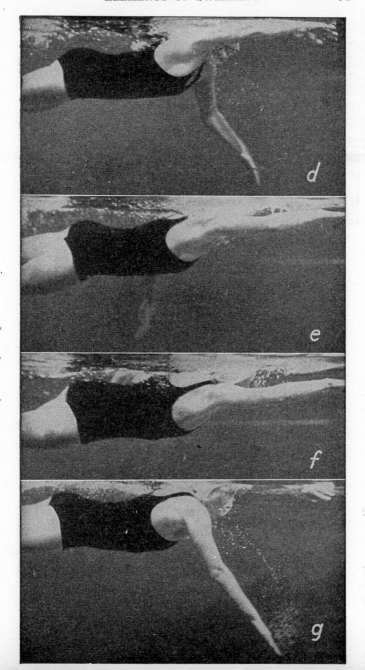

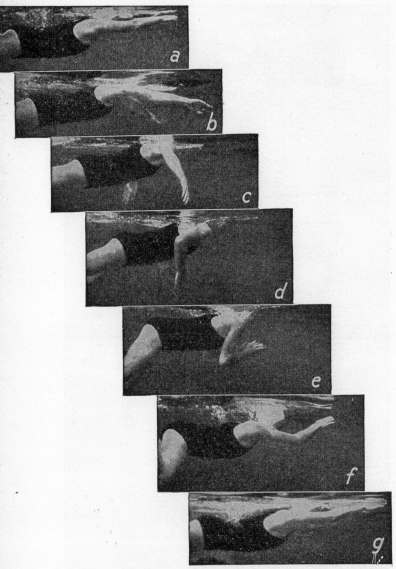

Fig. 29.—Detail of arms in breast stroke.

tion. These movements are timed so as to have the hands meet in front of the neck or chest. At this point the top arm becomes the propelling member as

Fig. 30.—One method of practicing arm strokes.

the under arm is recovered forward and returns to its original position; i. e., the under arm fully extended forward and the top arm extended in like manner along the side. In establishing this timing, if two things are kept constantly in mind, it is made relatively simple. First, the fully extended position of the arms, the under one to the front and the top to the rear, is the beginning and the ending of every stroke. The learner must return to this position at the completion of each stroke before the next one is begun. Secondly, the hands in mid-stroke must meet in the vicinity of the neck. If these two principles are adhered to, the arms will be synchronized no matter how they deviate from the correct track. This is a very ingenious method of using the arms in swimming. In essence it can be called a relay stroke in that the under arm delivers its thrust and then passes it on to the top arm to continue while it (the under arm) gets back into position to start another stroke. (See Fig. 27).

Use of Arms in Hand-over-hand Stroke.—Of all the names applied to stroking movements this is one of the most accurately descriptive. It is, as indicated by the name, an alternate over arm stroke in which the hands follow each other through the water at regular intervals and are recovered by lifting and sweeping or swinging forward beyond the head.

In the starting position for this stroke, one arm is extended beyond the head and directly in line with the eyes. At the beginning of the stroke the hand is allowed to drift down to a depth of four to six inches. At this point the hand catches the water and is pulled vigorously backward directly beneath the body to the vertical, with the arm bent somewhat at the elbow. Beyond the vertical the pull begins to diminish and the hand is allowed to drift back to the thigh. The recovery is made by rotating the hand until the thumb is turned downward and with a quick lift and bend of the elbow the forearm is drawn up and out of the water. As soon as the hand is above the surface the whole arm is thrust smartly forward and with the elbow still high the forearm is flung beyond the head and plunged beneath the surface as it is extended. In the co-ordinated use of two arms it may be stated broadly that they are alternate in their action although in the various styles of swimming in which this stroke is employed, the relationship between them may vary greatly. The learner must exercise care in the recovery to keep the elbow high and to have the hand enter the water smoothly allowing the arm to follow.

The full extension is not completed until the hand is well under water. (See Fig. 28).

Use of Arms in the Breast Stroke.—It is to be deplored that no descriptive term is in use aptly to describe the sweeping parallel movements of the arms as they are employed in certain styles of swimming. The breast stroke is descriptive enough of the use of the arms in swimming on the breast but when a similar stroke is employed in swimming on the back, its range and recovery movements may be quite different and it is no longer the breast stroke even though in principle it is the same. If there is any one term that may fitly describe this means of propulsion it is "broad stroking," implying as it does wide, sweeping movements of the arms but unfortunately it is not in common use and cannot be employed. (See Fig. 29).

In the front horizontal position the arms are held fully extended palms down in front of the face. The catch is made by rotating the hands until they are back to back and pressing outward against the water. Immediately, as a continuation of the previous movements, they are swept out slightly downward and back in a vigorous circling movement. This sweep is continued with straight arms until shoulder level is reached. At this point the elbows are bent and the hands sliced inward, thumbs foremost to a position in front of the chest, as the upper arms continue to circle until the elbows touch the sides. Then the hands, palm down and thumb to thumb, are extended and returned to the starting position. Identical movements are made with both arms simultaneously.

Learning Process for Arm Strokes.—The learning process for all arm strokes is quite similar to that of leg strokes. First, on land, the movement of a single arm is analyzed and practiced slowly to attain correctness and control. Then both arms are synchronized and the co-ordination of the two parts established. When this is accomplished the movements are made in series until the action becomes semi-automatic and a sense of rhythm is attained. Later the strokes are practiced in water breast-deep. Here the analysis of single arm movements is eliminated but practice of the co-ordinated arm movements is continued. For practice of the breast and hand-over-hand strokes the body is bent and the arms extended forward. For the practice of the side stroke, the body is bent forward and inclined somewhat to the side. The effectiveness of the pull may be measured by the tendency to draw the learner off balance. Finally, some artificial support is used for the feet while the arm strokes are practiced in the swimming position. (See Fig. 30).

At this point, before any co-ordinated style of swimming is attempted, it is advisable for the novice to check back on what has been accomplished. For some time, although he has concentrated on the mastery of these basic factors in swimming, he is still unable to swim a standard stroke, and yet many things have been accomplished. He has overcome fear of the water and has learned to modify his respiration to fit different conditions. He has mastered the basic principles of buoyancy, balance and propulsive movements. He has learned to float, to "fin" and to scull. He has learned three basic ways of using the legs and three more of using the arms. In fact, he has equipped himself with everything he needs to swim in any style he may select. This process may be likened to the building of a house. First, the builder must have his

materials and a plan. Then, he must lay his foundation and, finally, erect his structure. If he has no
plan, if he lacks certain materials, if his foundations
are insecure, his work will be makeshift, his finished
product will be uncertain and it will surely fail him
when most needed. At least, he will have small
faith in its ability to stand a crucial test. It is hardly
necessary to carry the simile further. The learner has
a plan, materials assembled and a solid foundation
laid if he has followed the foregoing instruction faithfully. On this he may build rapidly and well the
accepted styles of swimming.

CHAPTER IV

STYLES OF SWIMMING

In determining the order in which the various swimming styles are represented scant consideration is given to the selection of a basic style out of which all others are developed progressively. There is no basic method, only fundamental principles as described heretofore. Likewise there is no factor governing progression in learning unless ease of execution and economy of effort may be said to govern the learning method. On these bases it is reasonable to believe that the simplest co-ordinations in the most comfortable positions come first and by the same token, that the more complex and more nearly continuous rhythms are to be mastered last. Where there is a natural relationship in certain swimming styles due to the employment of similar stroking movements, it is logical that these styles should be grouped. Thus for example, the side stroke, the side overarm and the trudgen belong quite naturally together and should be learned in sequence.

Likewise, no consideration is given to the determination of the relative efficiency of swimming styles since there is no single standard which can be applied to all. Efficient use of any style is governed first, by the adaptability of the individual to that style and consequently, the extent of his mastery of it and secondly, by the uses to which it is put. The important thing is, at this point, that the novice is now equipped with a series of disciplined movements of arms and legs which are to be combined in the various styles of swimming. Confronted with the nine accepted styles or "strokes," the question will arise "which of these is to be undertaken first and what plan will be followed in learning them progressively?" In the purely mechanical aspect the answer is quite simple and on the basis of relative complexity of co-ordinations a learning sequence is now given. This is, however, by no means an arbitrary progression; it is only suggested, because of the variability of the human factor. Too often has it been noted that a novice having difficulty with a simple co-ordination, when switched to a much more complicated mechanical movement, has accomplished it with relative ease.

Categories of Strokes.—Styles of swimming fall quite naturally into four successive groups. First, there are the styles which employ only a paired movement of the arms and a like movement of the legs. As the arms make identical movements simultaneously and the legs are employed likewise, the co-ordination is composed of only two parts, a stroke with the arms and a stroke with the legs. The styles of swimming classified in this group are the commonly termed Elementary Back Stroke, Breast Stroke, and Inverted Breast Stroke. In the second group are placed the swimming styles in which the arms are stroked independently while the legs are employed in a paired movement. In these the co-ordination of three distinct motions are involved. The swimming styles in this category are those commonly called the side stroke, the overarm side stroke and the trudgen. The third classification covers those styles of swimming in which, even though the movements are similar, the arms and legs are stroked independently thereby involving the co-ordination of four parts. The crawl and the back crawl are thus classified. Lastly, there is a single style of swimming, the trudgen crawl, in which there are five distinct stroking motions to co-ordinate. As in the crawl, the arms and legs operate independently and, in addition, a paired leg movement is used at regular intervals in the stroke.

Before discussing these styles of swimming in detail and giving a learning formula for each it can be restated that the order in which they are given may not necessarily be the order in which they are to be mastered. It may not even be necessary to master all the stroking movements of the legs and arms before taking up the co-ordinated swimming styles. If the learner chooses for example, to develop the scissors stroke of the legs and the side stroking motion of the arms and to proceed directly to the side stroke no harm is done, certainly, and it may be easier for him, but he will find if he elects to follow that with the development of the overarm side stroke and the trudgen he will inevitably be handicapped in his progress until he has returned to fundamental stroking movements and mastered the overhand motion of the arms.

Elementary Back Stroke.—This is a very simple and easily mastered style of swimming apparently, of great antiquity since the first swimming book of which there is any record (Colymbetes, by Winman, 1537), mentions it as one of the three known methods of swimming at that time. That it was done in a variety of ways and that it evolved into the combination of movements now employed is evidenced by the descriptions of it given in many books on swimming during the past three or four hundred years.   About the only portion of the stroke on which early writers agreed, however, was the position on the back.   Some stated that the legs alone should be used, others described arm movements separately but neglected to say anything about putting together (co-ordinating) the arms and legs.   It was not until comparatively modern times that an effective co-ordination was evolved and taught.

The elementary back stroke is primarily a resting stroke to be resorted to whenever it becomes necessary to allow tired muscles to relax and recover, and to permit of deep and uninterrupted respiration, after strenuous effort.   It is useful, also, in levelling off in a back horizontal position from the vertical.   Unlike motionless floating, this stroke enables the swimmer to make slow but sustained progress in the resting position. The leg portion of the stroke, if strong, becomes an exceedingly useful factor in one type of swimming rescue in life saving.

The body, in this stroke, is placed in a back horizontal position, completely submerged with the exception of the face.   The back is flat or slightly rounded and the chin is tucked well into the throat.   The legs and hips are carried somewhat lower than the head and shoulders and all strokes of arms and legs including recovery movements are made beneath the surface.

The legs employ a breast stroke thrust in the inverted position.   The arms are used in the broad or breast stroke fashion, modified to suit the inverted position.   From a position fully extended along the sides, the hands are drawn toward the shoulders, palms in contact with the body throughout, elbows remaining as close to body as possible.   When the hands reach the shoulders they are rotated until the fingertips point outward. At this point the arms are immediately and fully extended at or a little above the shoulder level when the palm of the hand and the inside of the arm catch the water and with a broad sweeping stroke,

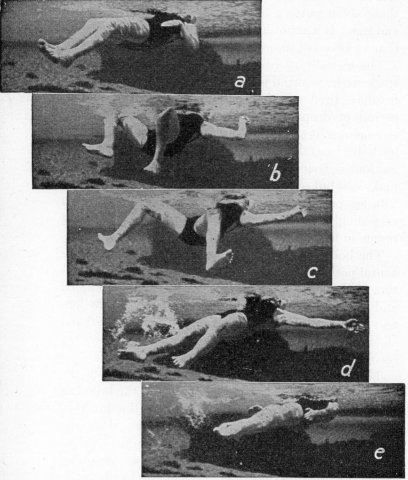

Fig. 31.—Co-ordination of elementary back stroke.

exactly as oars are pulled in boating, are pressed vigorously back and inward until they again reach the starting position.

The co-ordination of the two paired movements can be termed progressive. In the starting position the legs are held close together and fully extended, the arms, as before stated, close to the sides. The hands start to draw along the sides and as they reach the shoulders, the feet are drawn toward the body in the recovery portion of the leg stroke. As the hands rotate and extend outward to stroking position, the legs also are rotated and extended to be ready for the catch. Simultaneously the catch is made with both arms and legs and both are swept back and around to finish in position for the next stroke. The recovery of the arms leads the recovery of the legs because it is a movement of slightly greater range and takes a little longer interval than the legs to reach the stroking position. At the completion of each full stroke the streamlined position is held and the body allowed to coast or glide an appreciable distance before the next stroke is begun. It is advisable to co-ordinate the breathing with the stroke at regular intervals. This is accomplished quite simply by inhaling through the mouth during the recovery portion of the stroke, exhaling through the mouth and nose during the thrusting and gliding portions of the stroke. (See Fig. 31).

The learning method for this and all other styles of swimming begins with the easy assumption of the horizontal position. It is best accomplished for this stroke by taking a crouched position in water waist deep with all but the head submerged. Gently the body is inclined backward and as the balance is lost a vigorous but steady thrust against the bottom is made

with the feet.   The back is then flattened as the legs
are straightened and the learner glides out on the
surface with momentum enough to permit going into
the stroke in an unhurried manner without submerging
the head.   This back push-off and the recovery to the
standing position has, of course, been practiced many
times until it is accomplished smoothly and easily.   It
may be varied by using front push-offs and rotating
turns of the body to the back-gliding position.   Checking back on the practice of legs and arms in pairs, it is
recommended that here in the learning process the
learner practice swimming with legs alone and subsequently with arms alone without artificial support
until he is capable of making sustained and comfortable progress with either.   Then only is he ready to
co-ordinate the two movements according to the
description given in the preceding paragraph.   At
first, progression by means of this stroke will not be
great nor very efficient but with continued practice
the strength of the adductor muscles on the inner side
of the thigh, so necessary for effective leg stroking in
this style of swimming, will be developed.   When this
is mastered the learner is ready for the next style of
swimming.   The elementary back stroke now becomes
the first of his repertoire of swimming styles to be used
as his swimming experience increases in meeting situations and needs as they develop to which this type of
swimming is particularly adapted.

Breast Stroke.—This style of swimming, as stated
in the introduction, first came into general use in
northern Europe.   At least, that is where it is first
described in the earliest swimming literature of which
there is any record.   For centuries it was considered
to be the only correct and civilized method of swim-

ming on the front and as such, it was assumed that by means of it, every beginner should be taught how to swim. This being our historic heritage, it is understandable why, even to this day, the idea persists in many countries and in the minds of many people that the process of mastering the art of swimming begins with this wholly artificial style. Indeed, within the present lifetime of comparatively young men, it may be remembered that this was the only learning method available to non-swimmers. In view of what is known now about learning how to swim, it is recognized that learning this co-ordinated style of swimming (or any other for that matter) is neither safe nor sound in practice until the learner is well grounded in fundamental principles.

The evolution of breast stroke swimming as evidenced by the descriptions of the stroke written progressively through four centuries of literary effort of this kind is most interesting. Ralph Thomas gives a very interesting survey of the steps whereby the modern style of swimming on the breast was evolved which is, unfortunately, too long to be quoted here. However, certain quotations from authors listed in his bibliography and others taken directly from early swimming authorities may serve to show how this style was evolved to its present form. Winman contents himself by writing of this method "to keep the palms of the hands together . . . put your hands to center of breast then stretch out as far as able . . . " Of the feet he wrote " . . . the feet are to be driven like oars." (Rather difficult to follow it is suspected, if anyone tried to learn the breast stroke from that description.) Then, when words failed him he took the easy way out by citing an example in nature and

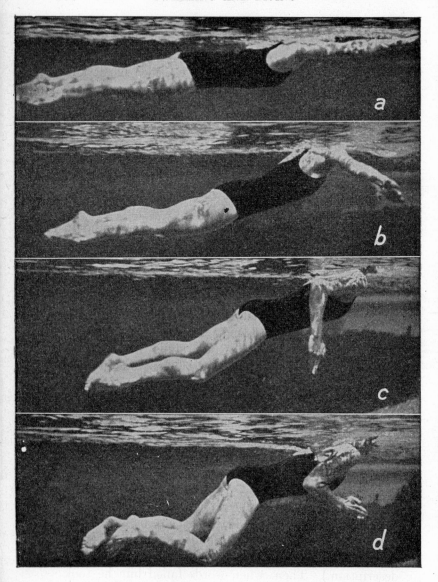

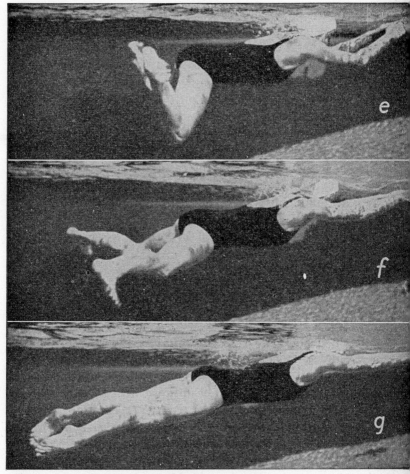

Fig. 32.—Co-ordinated breast stroke.

wrote " . . . you will learn best if you diligently watch how frogs swim with their hind feet . . . ," thereby demonstrating, if his observation was correct, that the breast stroke leg thrust was delivered at that time, backward and outward with the sole of the foot. Digby, 1587, apparently knew even less about it than

Winman, witness this description. "Raise your legs from the bottom," he wrote, "and expand them together by shooting them out, then stretch out your hands before you and expand them when extended; then bring them back again to your breast and strive to swim carefully and spiritedly, first with your feet and then with your hands, and you will be able to go on comfortably as long as you like." It is strange that a contemporary of Shakespeare could have found words so inadequately descriptive of the idea he sought to convey. It may be concluded from examination of the swimming literature of the 17th and 18th centuries that the arm portion of breast stroke swimming remained fairly constant as a wide sweeping, contracting and extending motion with but one change; i. e., about 1846 the hands which previously had been thrust forward palm to palm were placed thumb to thumb, palms down. In the latter part of the 18th century (1773), Benjamin Franklin in commenting on some experiments he was making at the time with swimming sandals wrote: "I was not satisfied because I observed that the stroke is partly given by the inside of the feet and the arches, and not entirely with the soles of the feet." This was the first written recognition of a fact that must have been hit upon accidentally by many good swimmers long before this time; namely, that the leg stroke was much more effective if made with a thrust of the sharply angled lower leg. Guts Muths in 1798 had apparently heard nothing of Franklin's experiment and conclusion for he wrote " . . . as they (the feet) go down they increase their distance (apart) and the external surfaces of the legs press against the water." A contemporary and countryman, however, (Salzman, 1800) refuted this by writing of the leg stroke " . . . the soles pushing against the water till brought close together in an extended position, which finishes the stroke." J. Frost, 1816, was the first swimming authority to repudiate that classic example of breast stroke swimming, the frog. He wrote "if you would be a swimmer, you must imitate the action of the frog, is founded on a gross mistake." Later in his work he gave a description of the true action. Clias in 1825 wrote in a footnote to his treatise on swimming that "the main advantage of swimming lies in this third part of the motion, that is, in the wedge." This is somewhat erroneous but refutes the frog action theory. Little was written about the co-ordination of the arm and leg portions of this stroke during this time, but in 1856 Stonehenge (J. H. Walsh) in a book titled British Rural Sports, wrote (in part) of breast stroke swimming "The action of the leg (read legs) is neither exactly synchronous with the arms nor precisely alternating with them, but for all practical purposes they may be considered as alternating. At the moment when the hands are fully extended (add forward), the legs have just completed their stroke and are drawn as quietly under the belly, while the arms are making their effort; upon the conclusion of which, or rather a little before its conclusion, the legs are violently thrust backward, outward and downward, completing the act in a shorter time, and with greater power than the arms have previously done." This is complicated to be sure but it betokens an awakened recognition of the fact that there must be a studied relationship between arms and legs if this style of swimming is to be done effectively.

Within recent years little change has been made in breast stroke swimming. Better and more accurate descriptions of arm and leg movements and of the co-ordination of parts have been written and the leg stroke has become a circular pressing movement; but, in principle, the style remains much as it was a hundred years ago.

The breast stroke has been for hundreds of years and will continue to be one of the most valuable and dependable styles of swimming in the swimmer's equipment. While it is not the fastest stroke it is undeniably the strongest and it can be used without special training for the event, to cover short or long distances. The ease with which recovery movements are made, the even distribution of work for the arms and legs in the propelling parts of the stroke and the long resting interval in the glide make sustained effort not only possible, but very enjoyable. In addition to this, it is the most social of swimming methods, particularly adaptable to paired or group swimming since, while swimming with the face above water, conversation is possible and the back is rarely turned toward anyone. When a swimmer is thrown into deep water accidentally, it is, of course, advisable to remove the outer clothing but if the distance to shore is short, it may be unnecessary to disrobe. Under such circumstances it will be readily discovered that breast stroke swimming is most useful. In under water swimming this style is almost invariably used and it is extensively employed either wholly or in part for some types of swimming rescue in life saving. In short, as the swimmer develops in water ability he will find an ever increasing number of uses for this stroke and, if it is well mastered, will come to regard it as a swimming method of great all around value.

Breast stroke swimming has the advantage of making it possible to swim with the face constantly above water, if desired, or it can be alternately raised for the inhalation and submerged for exhalation in the long glide. No matter which is used, the breathing is rhythmic and co-ordinated with the stroke. In the first case, the inhalation is taken in through the mouth during the pull of the arms and the exhalation takes place in the gliding portion of the stroke. In the second case a little difference is observed. As the finish of the long glide is approached while there is still some headway, the face is lifted from the water and the inhalation started. This is continued as the arms are pulled until a sufficient supply of air is taken, when the face is again immersed and the exhalation started and continued slowly through the leg thrust and the glide.

The stroking movements of the arms and legs have already been described and, supposedly, mastered. These paired movements are now to be fitted together to make up a complete stroke so co-ordinated that the effort will produce comfortable and continuous progress through the water.

The front horizontal position is assumed with head and shoulders at the surface and the body angling gently downward until the heels are about eight to twelve inches below the surface. The arms are fully extended in front of the head and the legs are extended in like manner to the rear. The back is somewhat flattened rather than arched. To begin the co-ordinated movement, the arms are pulled to the sides horizontally. As they approach the shoulder level, the feet begin to draw in the recovery portion of the leg stroke and as the arms are recovered and returned to the starting position, the legs are lashed out and around to return to their starting position where a glide of an appreciable distance is made. There are two keys to this combined stroke which, if noted and followed, make it almost impossible to co-ordinate the stroke incorrectly. First, the arms should not be pulled beyond the shoulder level; second, when the arms are extended forward, the legs are extended to the rear. The stroke is begun and ended in this position and the next stroke is never taken until this position is assumed at the completion of the preceding stroke. (See Fig. 32).

It has been noted frequently among novices in breast stroke swimming that, no matter how well it is co-ordinated, the stroke seems weak and the arm and leg portions poorly related to each other. This may be and frequently is due to lack of strength in the muscles on the inner sides of the thighs and nothing can overcome this lack of strength but continued practice. That this weakness may be due, however, to faulty body position is a fact not generally recognized. There is a tendency to carry an arched back through the entire stroking movement, whereas it should be used only in the glide. All leg thrusts originate in the muscle groups of the middle third of the body so as to get a maximum of power in the thrust, the big trunk muscles must do their part. The worst possible situation for employment of such muscles is that in which a deep arch of the spine is maintained throughout the leg stroking movement. Therefore, when the legs are drawn toward the body, the spine should be bowed upward a little and when the legs are swept back and pressed together, by the very action of flattening the spine the most effective use of the trunk muscles is made possible. To illustrate this point, a parallel athletic action may be cited. A football player kicking from placement would not think of advancing to the ball, stiffly erect with a deep arch in his back for he knows from experience that his kicking effort would be a sorry one. To get a maximum of power behind his "boot," he advances in a forward half-bending position and as his toe meets the ball, he adds to the kicking swing of the leg a vigorous straightening of the trunk as he "follows through." He operates on the same principles as the good breast stroker.

The learning process for breast stroke swimming can, and frequently does, begin with the use of some artificial support such as suspension in a sling, support on waterwings or hand support either under the chin, or by the back of the bathing suit; but because of uncertain equilibrium and the general cumbersomeness of the apparatus or method employed, the learner may find it quite difficult to concentrate on establishing the proper co-ordination. It is far better to use a learning method in which the novice, relying wholly on his buoyancy and natural sense of balance, can give all his attention to the stroke. This may be started on land. Standing on one foot and using a hand hold on a wall, back of a chair or some firm support, the learner can practice the co-ordination of the arm and leg of one side and then, facing about, can repeat the process on the other side. This may be repeated in sequence until the co-ordination is established and until it has become a semi-automatic action. In the water it is best practiced by starting with the long glide in the face floating position. Using the momentum of the glide and with the face still buried in the water, one completely co-ordinated movement is attempted which finishes in another long glide. Two complete strokes are tried next, emphasizing the glide between them.

If this practice takes place in a pool or on a beach where a natural objective may be selected, it is helpful to the novice to note what distance can be covered toward it first, with a glide and a single stroke, then with two and later in series limited only by the capacity to hold the breath. The co-ordination itself is governed by the words PULL (of the arms) THRUST (of the legs) and GLIDE and in co-ordinating the whole stroking movement the glide is of great importance. Only after the co-ordination is well established is it advisable to fit in correct breathing.

Inverted Breast Stroke.—The inverted breast stroke was evolved apparently as a more effective method of swimming on the back than the elementary form of back stroke previously described. It is, as the name indicates, the breast stroke turned upside down, differing only in the position of the body and an arm stroke of somewhat greater range. The strokes of arms and legs are practically alternating, so that the stroke finishes in a glide with the arms extended beyond the head. In this it differs from the elementary back stroke in which the glide is taken with the arms closed and extended along the sides. (See Fig. 33).

In the inverted breast stroke the arms are swept out and back almost to the sides instead of stopping the pull at shoulder level as in the breast stroke. For this reason, the recovery of the legs to stroking position is delayed a bit longer and there is a slightly more pronounced interval between the stroke of the arms and the stroke of the legs. The arms are recovered as gently as possible by drawing along the sides under water and extending them beyond the head.

Apparently the first swimming authorities to give this method of swimming any really serious thought

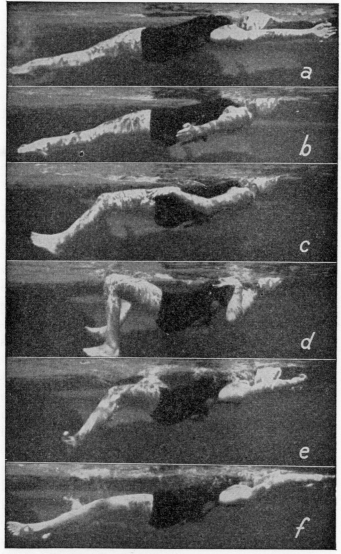

Fig. 33.—Co-ordination of inverted breast stroke.

and consideration were Sinclair and Henry ("Swimming," Badminton Library, 1894). The motivation for turning their attention to it was apparently its usefulness in life saving. Under "Swimming on the Back" several methods of back swimming are discussed. One essential point of difference, however, from the previous description of the inverted breast stroke, is given by them. Instead of recovering the arms beneath the surface they advocated for fast swimming on the back, a recovery above the surface either with a semi-circular sweep of straight arms or the bent-elbow draw and fling. This method in time became the racing stroke for swimming on the back and has only recently been superseded by the back crawl. Known as the European back stroke it persisted for years and even now is seen occasionally in competition. The recovery of the arms over the surface undoubtedly enables the swimmer to move more rapidly through the water but it is far less comfortable than the inverted breast stroke with arms recovered beneath the surface.

It is interesting to note that in Sinclair and Henry's time some speed swimmers were using alternate stroking of the arms with the breast stroke kick as a means for attaining greater speed. Later this arm stroke was used with the scissors of the legs and the way was open when the flutter kick came in, for the development and use of the back crawl. The inverted breast stroke as first described, however, still has a variety of uses to which it can be put and is a valuable addition to the category of strokes employed by anyone who wishes to call himself an all-around swimmer.

Side Stroke.—Evidence of the origin and subsequent development of this style of swimming leaves little room for doubt that it was a direct outgrowth of breast stroke swimming. In the experience of any swimmer, when the breast stroke is employed continuously over a considerable distance, it may be noted, especially if the face is carried above the surface, that there is a tendency to turn the head to one side or the other to relieve the strain on the muscles of the upper portion of the back and the nape of the neck. Inevitably it follows, that the axis of the shoulders is tilted and one shoulder is advanced thereby, throwing the body on the side and advancing the stroke of one arm to a position beyond the head while the other arm strokes on the side to which the face is turned. If this position is held persistently the arm stroking movement is changed to allow for a glide on the forward extended arm. The legs will continue to use the breast stroke movement but with lessened efficiency. The style is thus changed to side-swimming with the breast stroke, a method employed by many swimmers to this day in the belief that they are swimming the side stroke. At this point in its evolution its connection with the breast stroke was lost; first, by the change in the arm portion which became the alternate relay pull described heretofore under fundamental strokes; and second, by the substitution of the scissors stroke of the legs for the breast stroke leg thrust. Thus developed new stroking movements to meet new conditions. For historical proof of this Ralph Thomas must again be cited as authority. In his book he states that prior to 1840 all evidence indicates that for swimming on the side the breast stroke was employed. At approxi-

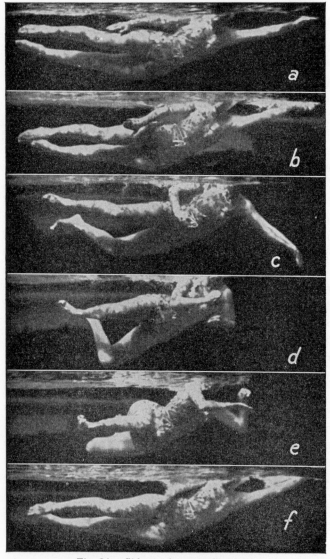

Fig. 34.—Side stroke co-ordination.

mately that date the stroke of the arms was changed to the alternate relay pull and very shortly thereafter (1840–1844) the scissors of the legs was evolved and the style of swimming called by him the English side stroke came into general use. As long as breast stroke movements were used there was a constant roll from the breast onto the side and back again but when the true side stroke came into use the swimmer remained constantly on the side.

It is unnecessary to list specific uses for this style of swimming when the whole stroke is employed. It can be stated simply that it is a comfortable steady stroke by which slow but certain progress is assured. Therefore, the swimmer may use it in any situation that the above qualifications may fit. When the leg portion of this stroke is considered, however, it is apparent that it has a very definite and important function for it is the basis of successful swimming rescue in American life saving. Two methods of carrying a victim, namely, the cross chest and the hair carries, require the scissors thrust of the legs for successful operation. A third method, the head carry, may usefully employ this same scissors in an inverted position. This requirement necessitates the development of a strong and smoothly co-ordinated "scissors" if the swimmer desires to learn how to save life in drowning accidents.

In this style of swimming the body remains constantly in a side horizontal position near the surface with the back flat. The side of the head is immersed and in line with the spine. The legs are carried somewhat lower than the head to insure efficient stroking against unbroken water. The stroking movements of arms and legs have already been described and presumably mastered. The combination of these strokes for effective side stroke swimming is accomplished as follows: In the starting position on the side, the lower arm is extended straight beyond the head, the cheek is rested on the extended shoulder. The upper arm is extended along the side with the palm resting on the thigh. The legs are extended backward, close together and with toes pointed. To begin the stroke the lower arm catches and starts to pull. As it approaches the vertical, the upper arm and the legs begin to recover and as the lower arm completes its pull and starts to bend upward to recover, the upper arm and the legs catch simultaneously, and drive through to complete the stroking movement, the lower arm meantime returning to its original extended position to take advantage of the long glide which follows upon the completion of the stroke. The breath is taken through the mouth during the pull of the lower arm and exhaled as the upper arm delivers its thrust and throughout the glide. (See Fig. 34).

In side stroke swimming, as in riding a bicycle, it is difficult to maintain the balance without momentum. Therefore, after the land drill, the next step in the learning process is to achieve balance on the side. This is best accomplished by practicing push-offs on the side, on the breast with a roll to the side position, and even on the back with a similar turn. When some sense of balance is secured by this practice, the swimmer may at once begin the practice of the co-ordinated stroke. Contrary to the practice employed in breast stroke swimming and swimming on the back, there can be no long gliding interval between every two strokes because in the early stages of learning the balance is so easily lost. At first, the stroking must be almost continuous and only after the balanced position is held automatically can there be any appreciable glide between strokes. However, the strokes should never be shortened or hurried as the two key positions governing the co-ordination must be definitely taken in each cycle of movements. The first or starting position with legs and upper arm fully extended to the rear and lower arm extended beyond the head, must always be returned to at the completion of one stroke before the next one is begun even though no glide is taken in that position. Likewise, midway of the combined stroke the palm to palm position of the hands and the spread posture of the legs must be taken definitely, as the second check on the co-ordination. In essence, the combined stroke is composed of two essential parts. The lower arm working alone, contributed some forward progress, it is true, but the chief function is to maintain momentum and balance while the breath is taken and the upper arm and the legs are recovered in preparation for their stroke. The major propulsive drive is then delivered by the upper arm and the legs working in combination. Thus the stroke becomes a minor effort with the lower arm followed by a major effort with the other limbs. Side stroke swimming is made up progressively of a PULL of the lower arm followed by a THRUST of the upper arm and the legs. After the combined stroke is mastered, the breathing and the glide may be added to perfect this style of swimming.

Overarm Side Stroke.—There has been some confusion in recent years concerning the name which properly applies to this style of swimming. It has been termed variously; the single overhand, single overarm, English overarm, English side stroke and overarm side

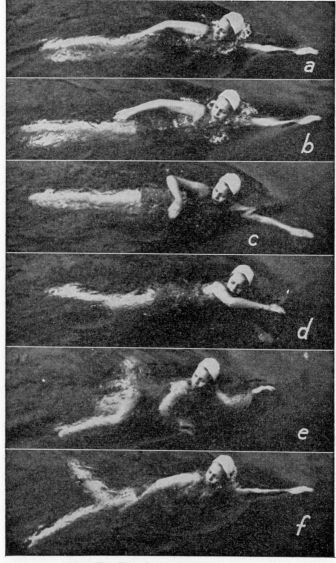

Fig. 35.—Overarm side stroke.

stroke. It is most frequently referred to as the English overarm stroke largely because of its origin. It is true that it had its origin and greatest development in England but as there is no other overarm side stroke it is referred to in England simply by that name and should be so termed.

The overarm side stroke is a natural variation of the side stroke and, doubtless, came into use at almost the same time. Thomas gives its date of origin as 1855 but it must have been used experimentally years before then, since the only change involved was to recover the upper arm over the surface, instead of beneath it, to reduce resistance. It was first described as a distinct style of swimming by Ralph Harrington in 1861. The overarm side stroke came into general use in England at about the same time that interest in competitive swimming quickened. The search for speedier strokes may or may not have been a factor in its evolution, but certainly this style of swimming was used by most of the swimming champions over a period of years which extended almost to the turn of the century. In the earlier years Davenport and Finney were among the best and speediest exponents of overarm side stroke swimming and they were followed by Nuttall, Evans and Tyers who held championships for many years.

With the advent of the trudgen style of swimming, overarm side stroke swimming began to fade as a speed stroke and when the crawl came in, it was quickly forgotten by competitive swimmers. Nevertheless, it has persisted as a graceful, easily accomplished swimming style which compares favorably with breast stroke swimming, for covering short or long distances at a moderate pace without too great expenditure of

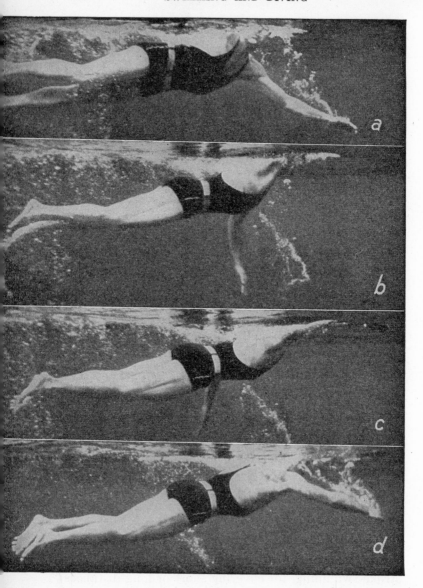

Fig. 36.—The trudgen.

energy.   Its rhythm and space-devouring thrusts and
glides make it a truly valuable swimming style for
covering long distances without particular training.

For example, a person having a boat sink beneath him
at a considerable distance from shore may, by alternately employing overarm side and breast stroke
swimming, make steady progress toward shore and
sustain the effort for a considerable period, by thus
conserving his energy.

The position of the body is the same as in side stroke
swimming and the legs are employed in the same kind
of scissors stroke. The arms alternate in the same
way but their range of movement is increased. The
lower arm in the overarm side stroke pulls vertically
fully extended, while the upper arm drawing and
recovering above water is extended to catch the water
at a point just beyond the forehead. The recovery of
the lower arm is practically the same as in the side
stroke. The upper arm recovery with the bent elbow
and trailing thumb is like the recovery in the basic
hand-over-hand stroke. The style may be swum
wholly on the surface or alternately above and below
it, depending upon the buoyancy of the swimmer and
the speed of the stroke. Heavy swimmers tend to
submerge the head as they near the end of the long
underarm pull and to emerge as the stroke is taken up
by the upper arm and the legs. In either case, the
integration of the breathing is the same; namely, to
inhale during the under arm pull and to exhale continuously through the remainder of the stroke. (Fig. 35).

The learning method for overarm side stroke swimming is merely an adaptation of the side stroke and a
continuation of its practice. The adaptation is begun
by practicing the recovery of the upper arm out of
water, with particular attention to securing relaxation
in the recovery and a clean entry of the hand. Then
the lower arm is straightened and its range increased.

The Trudgen Stroke.—It is interesting to note that the only style of swimming named after a swimmer was not originated by him nor is it as employed today, the stroke swam by the man who gave it a name.

John Trudgen, according to a biographical note by Thomas " . . . went to Buenos Ayres in 1863. While there he learnt 'to trudge' from the natives." So he did not originate the stroke. At another point in his book Thomas writes, "Surely no man ever obtained so much fame for so little as Trudgen. The inventor of the English side stroke is unknown, but Trudgen will always be in evidence, from the accidental circumstance of his winning a sprint race with the South American Indian stroke." The circumstance which brought this about is interesting and worthy of full explanation, because there has been so much confusion concerning the origin of the "trudgen." Quoting from Sinclair and Henry's work on Swimming "the account of an eye witness of Trudgen's first race in England is revealing." The following in turn is a quotation from Watson in the Swimming Record of 1873. He said, "A surprising swimmer carried off the handicap—we allude to Trudgen: this individual swam with both arms entirely out of water, an action peculiar to Indians. His time was very fast, particularly for one who appears to know but little of swimming, and should he become more finished of style, we shall expect to see him take a position almost second to none as a swimmer. I question, indeed, if the swimming world ever saw a more peculiar stroke sustained throughout a 160 yards race. I have seen many fast exponents retain the action for some distance, but the great exertion compels them to desist, very much fatigued. In Trudgen, however, a totally opposite state of things existed; for here we had a man swimming apparently easy, turning very badly and when finished, appearing as though he could have gone another 80 yards at the same pace. His action reminds an observer of a style peculiar to the Indians: both arms are thrown partly sideways, but very slowly, and the head kept completely above water."

Henry, remarking further about Trudgen's style wrote, "The body is lifted at each stroke and at each swing of the arms seems to be hurled forward, a considerable swirl of the water occurring as each movement is finished." Neither of these quotations describe the leg portion of the stroke but that of Henry does give a clue. The "hurling forward of the body at each stroke of the arms" and the high position of the head and shoulders can mean only one thing; that the legs using a combination of breast and side stroke kick were delivering a thrust with each arm stroke. This is substantiated by evidence displayed among some native South Americans and West Indians who use this double kick with the hand-over-hand arm stroke even now. With it some of them can swim very rapidly for short distances but it is an exhausting method.

The speed swimmers of England were evidently impressed by Trudgen's style of swimming and began almost immediately to experiment with it for short distances. Because they were for the most part overarm side stroke swimmers, it was only natural that they should seek to evolve a hand-over-hand style out of the stroke in which they were well-practiced, rather than to imitate Trudgen's style slavishly. In so doing, they evolved the method by which the trudgen is swum at present. In the practical evolution of the stroke all that these early swimmers did was to swim the overarm side stroke with a roll onto the breast which permitted them to recover the under arm over the surface. Later, the top arm reach to the catch was extended well beyond the head in the roll and the scissors of the legs narrowed until the top leg merely trailed and the lower leg executed its thrust largely from the knee downward. Finally the side position was largely eliminated, especially in sprinting. Some trudgen swimmers, having good buoyancy, even eliminated the leg stroke entirely, thereby removing the negative recovery movement of the leg as a check to speed.

The trudgen is a powerful and, relatively, mechanically efficient style of swimming which has, when needed, considerable speed. When properly co-ordinated and swum correctly it can be used for short or long distances. Its best use is perhaps, as a relief stroke for crawl swimmers who may wish to continue swimming a hand-over-hand style. When the flutter kick begins to lose its propulsive drive because of tiring leg muscles, it is the common rather than the rare occurrence for crawl stroke swimmers to fall back upon the trudgen either wholly or in combined form.

In discussing the evolution of the trudgen it was reasonably well analyzed but it may be wise again to describe the stroke. Briefly, it is a combination of the hand-over-hand method of employing the arms in combination with a single scissors stroke of the legs which by adding a considerable roll of the body has evolved from the overarm side stroke. The arm on one side strokes along but on the other, the arm pull is combined with a scissors of the legs. Theoretically, this unbalanced thrust should result in uneven propulsion but in actual practice, if the momentum is properly employed in a substantial glide, progress is almost continuous. The breath is taken, as usual, at the highest point of the stroke which, in this case, is during the pull of the single arm. The exhalation takes place during the combined stroke of the other arm and the legs. (See Fig. 36).

The learning method as a step in the progressive development of swimming styles is quite simple. The learner can best start by swimming the overarm side stroke for a few strokes to gain the rhythm and then modify it, by rolling onto the breast as the upper arm reaches forward, to clear the under arm for an over water recovery. Gradually the roll is lessened and the leg scissors narrowed until the stroke is swum almost entirely on the breast with rotation only sufficient to clear the arms for the over water recovery and to breathe.

Back Crawl.—Almost all swimmers regardless of their experience have at some time or another in the water turned on the back and with a vigorous churning up and down thrash of the legs kicked their way along. Consciously or otherwise and in many instances, long before the crawl was known they were swimming the leg portion of the back crawl. So, it was only natural when the crawl came into use for swimmers to invert it and combine the leg action in that position long familiar to them with the reverse action of the hand-over-hand stroke. Again it was the competitive swimmers who first realized its value for racing and contributed most to its development and refinement. While it is still referred to commonly as the racing back stroke, there is a growing recognition of its value as a remarkably efficient style of swimming suitable for

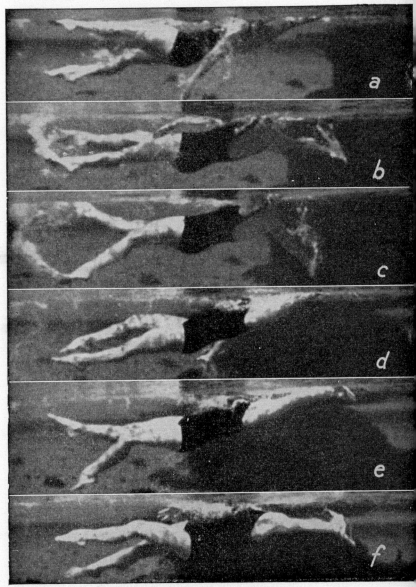

Fig. 37.—The back crawl.

short or long distances. The fact that it is more comfortable and less taxing physically than the crawl contributes also to its ever-increasing popularity.

In swimming the inverted crawl, a position is taken on the back with the head in line with the spine and the chin tucked well into the neck. The hips are lowered slightly to bring the feet far enough below the surface to get good traction. The flutter kick is used in the six-beat crawl cadence with a slightly greater bend at the knee and consequent deeper leg stroke. The emphasis is placed on the downward and backward pedal thrust and on the lifting or "spooning" upstroke. Lack of flexibility in the ankles and resultant indifferent traction may be offset by rolling slightly and putting in two major beats as in the trudgen-crawl. For maximum efficiency, however, there should be little or no roll to the body. It is necessary to adapt somewhat the hand-over-hand stroke to the dorsal position for successful use. The catch is made beyond the head and four to six inches beneath the surface. The arm is then pulled out, down and back to the thigh at a depth directly limited by the flexibility of the shoulder. As the hand nears the thigh, the thumb is rotated inward until the palm faces out. To recover the arm, the elbow is lifted to shoulder height as the forearm is withdrawn. Immediately, and as a continuation of this movement, the upper arm is allowed to fall back beyond the head and the forearm is flung in flail fashion to a fully extended position on the surface. The recovery is in line with the shoulders and made rapidly so that one arm is always extended as the other is completing its pull. It is advisable to breathe rhythmically, inhaling at the high point of one arm stroke and exhaling continuously through the remainder of the arm cycle, but if it is necessary to interrupt the breathing, to blow spray from the face or to hold the breath it is not necessary to break the rhythm of the stroke as it is in the crawl in similar circumstances.   (See Fig. 37).

Practice in the back crawl is begun in shallow water with the flutter kick first.   Supported only by the hands resting on the bottom the body is kicked to the horizontal in the face-up position.   The leg strokes may then be developed rhythmically and in sequence until they can be done comfortably and with some efficiency as evidenced by the tendency to drive the body backward.   Two methods of practicing the kick in a free swimming position are recommended; first, to rest the back of the head on the end of a kick-board with the hands grasping the sides of the board beyond the head; second, to stretch the arms beyond the head palms up and thumbs clasped.

The arm stroke is best practiced by lying on the surface with the feet supported by a fellow swimmer. In this position the pull and recovery of the arms can be "felt out" and their co-ordination established. Later, with a floating support for the feet, the arm stroke can be practiced in a free swimming position. Co-ordination of arms and legs is established and the stroke perfected in much the same way as in the crawl; i. e., over measured courses of ever increasing length until ten to twenty lengths of a pool or two hundred to five hundred yards of open water can be covered with ease.

Crawl Stroke Swimming.—As stated previously in the discussion of the flutter kick, the crawl is a distinctly modern style of swimming involving a new method of employing the legs.   Evidence has been

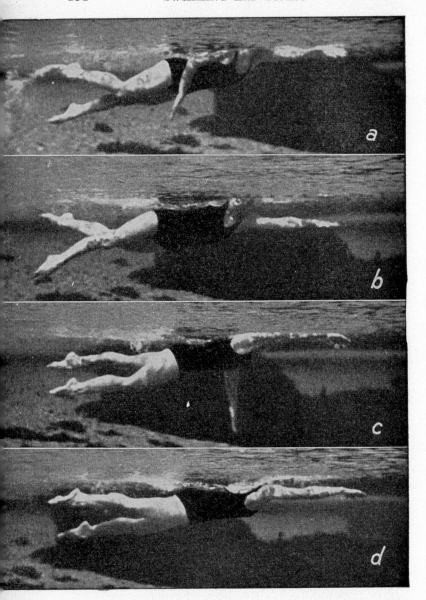

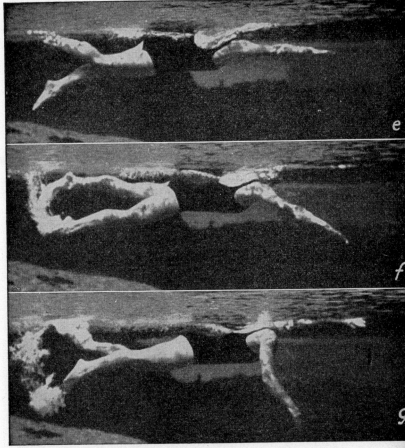

Fig. 38.—The crawl.

given many times of an historical background for this stroke covering a period of thousands of years. Yet it is a matter of doubt as to whether it can be said that the Assyrians, the Greeks and the Romans swam the crawl as it is now swum any more than it can be said that Trudgen swam a crawl. A careful study of the facsimiles of the bas-reliefs from the Nimroud Palace reveals only two things about the stroke the Assyrians used; first, that they swam hand-over-hand and second, that the legs show no evidence of undulating in the vertical thrash employed. This may be due to the highly formalized crudity of the sculpture but it is more reasonable to believe that Assyrian warriors swam with the human stroke kick (striking the water with a vigorous beat of the shin and instep) or, (less likely) they swam with the quadruped stroke of the legs; i. e., pressing the soles of the feet alternately backward against the water. The only references in early swimming literature to any stroke which at all resembles the modern crawl are to be found in two boys' handbooks of sports published about 1860. The Boy's Own Book of Sports, Birds and Animals published in New York by Leavitt and Allen, with no date of publication and attributed to no author describes a swimming method known as creeping and recommends it as "very serviceable to get clear of weeds." Presumably the book was published in the late 1850's. The other reference is found in George Forrest's book entitled "A Handbook of Swimming and Skating," published in London in 1858. He, also, describes a stroke called "creeping" and the gentle fluttering movements of straight legs as a useful means of enabling a swimmer to extract himself from weeds. These are the only references apparently to a method of employing the legs which was a direct fore-runner of the modern crawl stroke flutter kick. It is remarkable that by unhappy accident, this method of extracting one's self from weeds was not continued in open water. If it had been tried, the world would not have had to wait a half century for the discovery of this remarkable style of swimming.

If it is stated that the Assyrians swam in a manner closely resembling the early Australian crawl swimmers the contention is undeniably correct. Both used the hand-over-hand arm stroke and the human kick. As stated, heretofore, the combination of movements described above were borrowed from the native swimmers in Ceylon. Alec Wickham was the first to copy the style but it remained for Richard Cavill, a noted Australian competitive swimmer to popularize its use. In due time it became known as the crawl stroke and because it was introduced to the swimming world from that country, it became widely known as the Australian Crawl. Three things were done to this combination of movements by the Australians which developed a style of swimming quite different from any employed before. For the first time an effort was made to synchronize the movements of the arms and legs in this style of swimming and a two beat stroke was the result. That is, the left arm and right leg worked together on one beat and the right arm and left leg on the next. Second, the arm stroke was much shortened in range to enable the swimmer to stroke more rapidly and third, for short sprints the face was laid in the water and lifted only when a breath of air was required. This last innovation is the only one of the three which has survived in the modern development of the crawl and is of far greater importance than was suspected at first.

When the Australian Crawl was brought to this country in 1904 it was immediately adopted by the foremost American swimmers of that time because of its superiority as a sprint swimming stroke. Its best performer and advocate was C. M. Daniels who doubled and then tripled the rhythm of the leg stroke with consequent increased speed. This involved narrowing the leg thrash and lengthening the arm stroke but the principle of lashing the water with the shin and instep on the downward thrust still governed the flutter kick and continued to do so until comparatively recent times. With six strokes of the legs to every cycle of the arms the rhythm was finally stabilized and this ratio is accepted as standard at present for the American Crawl. This was the first change in the Australian stroke made by swimmers in this country and while it made of the crawl a faster sprinting stroke it did not, apparently, increase its efficiency in any other way. Evidence of the limitations of the American version of the crawl is shown by the fact that even many "top-flight" swimmers employ a trudgen-crawl at distances greater than two hundred meters. It is among those swimmers only who have mastered a flexible undulation of the legs combining efficient traction and relaxation between kicks thereby making possible a sustained effort, that a true crawl is swum.

It is unfortunate that the American Crawl was given to the swimming world as a sprinting stroke. Like every other new style of swimming it was immediately siezed upon and imitated by swimmers everywhere with a fine disregard of the principles involved in skilled performance. Almost any swimmer could, by lowering the head and flailing the water windmill fashion, swim ten or fifteen yards at a faster pace than ever before and call it crawl swimming, despite the fact that the effort could not be sustained for any considerable distance because of inevitable exhaustion. It has been the history of the crawl that only those swimmers who painstakingly followed the principles of mastery of individual stroking movements and co-ordination of all components of this style of swimming have realized its full possibilities.

If any one factor is selected as outstanding in demonstrating its usefulness it should be that of mechanical efficiency. The swimmer can get better results in distance covered and elapsed time for the energy expended in the crawl than in any other style of swimming. This is not the whole story, however. In situations where a sudden burst of speed is necessary such as making for shore when in peril or reaching a drowning person quickly, the crawl is acknowledged to be the stroke to use for such occasions. When time is a factor to be considered in long swims, the use of the crawl or its "blood brother" the trudgen-crawl may mean the difference between life and death. For example, if a swimmer in the open sea by some accidental means is faced with the necessity of covering a considerable distance to shore before the ebb of the tide sets out, he will find that the crawl may take him in where a slower stroke might leave him still at some distance from the beach when the ebb comes. Added to these examples of usefulness are the physical values of such a finely co-ordinated rhythmic and continuous action. The crawl may be said to be the acme of all styles of swimming.

If it is stated that the crawl is made up of a hand-over-hand stroke of the arms and a flutter kick of the legs, it would be only a partial truth. Such a limited description of the stroke has governed its development for thousands of swimmers in the past and has been responsible in large measure for much of the poor and mediocre swimming done in its name. It is true that the crawl is composed of four independent movements

grouped generally as described heretofore but because
it is so finely co-ordinated it merits complete analysis
as a step in the learning method.

The position of the body in the crawl is, of course,
near the front horizontal. It should be assumed
in the most comfortable manner possible consistent
with the maintenance of equilibrium and yet allow for
ease and efficiency in stroking. A number of body
positions are commonly taken by swimmers. Some
swim with a pronounced arch to the spine, others swim
with flat backs. Many swim with the whole body
angled slightly downward and backward while a few
keep the trunk level and angle the legs downward.
These differences are based on individual physical
structure, type of musculature and buoyancy. Every
swimmer must find for himself a position in which
he is well-balanced and able to get the best traction
and be governed only by the necessity for keeping
the head in line with the spine, breathing rhythmically
and freely and placing the feet far enough beneath the
surface to stroke efficiently.

In the crawl, the hand-over-hand arm stroke attains
its highest degree of refinement. In ordinary use this
stroke is customarily divided into two parts for
analysis; namely, the pull and the recovery but in its
most efficient form in the crawl there are studied movements or positions to be considered. Entry is followed
by extension and the catch is delayed. The recovery
is more rapid. To visualize this process clearly it is
advisable to study the action of a single arm, first.
For all practical purposes, the arm cycle may be
divided into three sections; the working part, in which
propulsive effort is made, the recovery which is a
negative movement as far as propulsion is concerned

and the resting portion which aids materially in
forward progress.   Starting with the forward extended
position of the arm, the hand is allowed to drift downward several inches below the surface as the body
rides over it by its own momentum. The catch is
then made and the stroke is pulled through with a
definitely bent elbow.   It should be a drawing rather
than a downward pressing effort. As the draw passes
the vertical the arm begins to relax and is allowed to
drift back to the thigh.   Then it is quickly drawn out
of the water with a high elbow and flung rather
than carried forward as rapidly as possible. The
entry of the hand is made just beyond the head while
the elbow is still high. As a continuation of this
recovery movement the arm is fully extended forward
beneath the surface and allowed to rest for an appreciable interval before the next stroke is begun.

When both arms are in operation the relationship
between them is very definite, even though they are
stroked independently. The recovery is made so
rapidly that one arm is always extended forward
while the other is pulling through. This procedure
allows the swimmer to glide on an extended arm
continuously, achieving thereby better equilibrium and
a position high in the water with little effort.

In the crawl the legs are, of course, employed in the
flutter kick.   Their action serve two purposes for most
swimmers; first to keep the body in a position at or
near the horizontal and second, to provide auxiliary
propulsion. The major portion of the drive will
come from the arms but the legs will definitely contribute something to the forward movement.

The combined action of arms and legs may be
likened in effect to that of a side-wheel steamer

equipped with an auxiliary propeller at the stern. Each power unit by itself would produce forward motion at a uniform rate, but the two working together produce an increased rate of progress, providing that their power application is so synchronized that one is not neutralizing the effect of the other. Unbalanced stroking is too often the cause of poor or indifferent crawl swimming. Most generally it is the application of too much power in stroking with the arms which upsets the balance of the stroke by rendering the action of the legs neutral or even negative in their action. The legs striving desperately to do their part, speed up their action, narrow the thrash and tighten the muscles thereby losing traction and tiring quickly. The key to the development of efficient crawl swimming, therefore, will be more than any other one thing, the careful relation of timing and application of power in the arm and leg strokes. (See Fig. 38).

In the crawl the head is held in line with the spine to preserve equilibrium, so the face is carried for the most part below the surface. This necessitates careful integration of breathing with the stroke and it will be found that the type of breathing learned in beginning swimming will have its greatest value in this stroke. It is important that regular exchange of air should be effected with the least possible disruption of rhythm in stroking and little or no loss of balance.

If it is assumed that the swimmer takes his air to the left, the procedure is as follows. When the right arm is extended forward in the gliding position, the face is rotated rather than lifted to the left until the nose and mouth are above the surface. A full inhalation is taken by mouth continuing until the recovering left arm by the action of its forward swing turns the face down and forward for the exhalation.

The swimmer will have mastered the fundamentals of the hand-over-hand stroke and the flutter kick long before this point is reached in his progression. His practice for the crawl will consist, therefore, first, of making the slight change in the relationship of the arms in the crawl and second, of fitting arms, legs and breathing together in one harmonious whole.

The arm stroke is practiced standing in breast deep water with the body inclined forward until correct spacing of strokes is achieved, then, with a floating support for the feet, the learner continues the practice slowly over a prescribed distance, "feeling out" the stroke. Only the recovery over water will be made rapidly during this practice. Tendencies to over-reach, to press instead of draw and to drop the shoulder too low will be observed and corrected as the arms get the "feel" of the stroke. Particularly is it necessary to check the tendency to catch and pull as the hand enters the water rather than to ride the extended arm for an appreciable interval before starting its pull.

Practice in breathing, quite logically, is fitted into the stroke at this point, as it is so closely related to the arm action and must be synchronized with it.

The whole stroke is best practiced between two fixed points from which a "push off" can be taken. A swimming pool offers the best practice field for crawl swimming. Working, at first, from side to side a distance of twenty-five, thirty, or thirty-five feet, a push-off will provide initial impetus. This is followed by a pick up of the flutter kick and then arms and breathing. In the first few attempts the rhythm may be lost almost as soon as it is acquired but, because the

distance is so short, it can be covered without changing
stroke and a fresh start can be made with another
push-off. Thus, continuously, widths are covered
with pauses at the sides only long enough to change
position or to analyze a fault and eliminate it, until
twelve to sixteen widths can be covered without a
break or change in stroke. Then the swimmer is
ready to try lengths (sixty or seventy-five feet), and
for the first time the stroke will have to prove its
effectiveness or lack of it. It must be swum slowly
at all times. If the swimmer has to speed up his
rhythm or change his stroke to keep going he should
stop and pull in to the side to take a fresh start. When
he can cover ten to twenty lengths at a moderate pace
with comparative ease and with no resting intervals
he is really swimming the crawl. After that the
development of endurance through training and practice will determine maximum distance and rate of
speed for the swimmer.

At no time in the learning process heretofore
described has there been any thought of developing
sprint swimming. Swimming the crawl at top speed
for short distances has no part in this swimming progression. That comes much later as a culmination of
speed efficiency. To introduce the sprint crawl with
its variations at this point in the progression would
seriously hinder the development of the crawl as a
useful and basic style of swimming.

The Trudgen-Crawl.—Many swimmers find it
impossible to sustain a true crawl stroke for any great
distance no matter how well they co-ordinate the
stroke or how assiduously they practice. In almost
every case it is due to ineffectiveness of the leg stroke.
This may result from lack of flexibility, especially in

the ankles; poor traction because of faulty angle of the foot or lack of foot area; or, lack of balance in the stroke as a result of undue emphasis on the arm portion of it. For these swimmers the trudgen-crawl offers a means of overcoming such handicaps.

Originally this stroke was developed out of the trudgen simply by adding four flutter kick beats after the scissors kick, in the interval during which the legs ordinarily trailed. In later years the process of development has been reversed and it is now customary to develop it from the crawl. This is often done quite unconsciously by the crawl swimmer by developing one or two major beats in his flutter kick as an ingenious method of compensating for his lack of power in the true crawl leg drive. If a single major beat is employed it is accomplished by rolling slightly to the breathing side and substituting a narrow slashing scissors kick for the first two beats and following it with four ordinary flutter kicks. In scissoring, the knees are drawn toward the body slightly and snapped out, back, and together as a means of relieving the tension on the thigh muscles. In the double trudgen-crawl, the first scissors is made in exactly the same manner as in the single trudgen-crawl, but it is followed by two flutter beats and a roll to the opposite side. The second scissors is taken on the fourth beat and followed by two more flutter kicks. Thus, slash, beat, beat, slash, beat, beat, becomes the correct rhythm. While this stroke is not as even or as rapid as the true crawl it does contribute to endurance and may be used quite satisfactorily by those who find the mastery of the true crawl difficult.

As the trudgen-crawl is merely the crawl with another type of kick added at regular intervals, the learning process is identical. The roll of the body will change the action of the arms slightly by causing the shoulders to dip but as this action develops almost automatically, no special concentration on accomplishing it is necessary.

Summary.—If this progression has been followed faithfully, the learner will have found that as he advanced step by step the mastery of swimming has become at once more difficult and easier; easier, because he has become ever more accustomed to the water and more difficult, because of the increased complexity of the co-ordinations. If not soundly grounded in fundamentals, he may have found that his swimming structure was weakened by an insecure member in his foundation. "A chain is only as strong as its weakest link," is a homely adage which applies to nothing more aptly than it does to swimming.

Progress may have been very uneven in the mastery of the various styles of swimming. One stroke may have been learned with comparative ease while proficiency in another proved most difficult to acquire. Preference for certain strokes is governed by the immeasurable human factor while mastery of many is governed wholly by the physical and mental flexibility of the swimmer and application to the learning process. The novice may content himself with the mastery of one category of swimming strokes and feel, quite logically, that he has achieved water locomotion, but he can never feel thoroughly at home in the water until he has developed enough watermanship to meet any and all water conditions as they may arise.

Again it may be stated as a truth, that, while it is possible for some persons to master natation without assistance, their progress will be much more rapid under the coaching of an expert instructor. For the vast majority expert analysis by a qualified instructor is a necessity for he alone may be able to detect false movements and assist in their correction.

Probably ninety out of every hundred persons who enter the water seeking to learn how to swim cherish the secret ambition of becoming perfect swimmers, yet when questioned as to what constitutes perfection in swimming very few can give a clear description of their aims. To the majority, it means mastery of all the things they have seen, heard, or read about in all branches of natation. Floating, swimming, diving, stunt swimming, under-water swimming and many other forms of aquatic activity are present in their minds in one splendid kaleidoscopic maze with no clear beginning, no thought of progression and no end. To some novices perfection means the ability to swim faster than anyone else. Others, with a more worthy conception of the term, consider it to be the real mastery of one or more swimming styles, but even this is insufficient. What, then, is the test of a perfect swimmer? In 1836 a Frenchman, Count de Courtivron wrote in a book he published on swimming:

"To be entitled to be so described (a perfect swimmer), which strictly should not be applied to any art or science or anything human, you must be able to swim in all situations, rest in one way or another, vary your attitudes and fear neither cramp, waves, weeds, nor whirlpools. The perfect swimmer must have a good constitution, be accustomed to the water, so as not to fear it however cold, and be ready to undertake the longest journeys and cross the most rapid rivers and streams . . . presence of mind which enables him to see dangers without concern, and to calculate the means of avoiding them, in fact that coolness and courage which is necessary more than anything else, to surmount every kind of peril."

Perfection in watermanship is well within the reach of all but a few of those who swim. It requires little more than patient application to rhythmic progressive development.

CHAPTER V

OTHER FORMS OF SWIMMING

Treading Water.—While the first literary reference to treading water occurs in Colymbetes (1538) in which it is described as the third mode of swimming, it was, without doubt, in use for many years prior to that time. For centuries it was considered to be merely a cumbersome method of swimming in an upright position. Extravagant claims were made for its military value in enabling soldiers to carry arms and equipment on their heads in traversing rivers and streams. As a means of locomotion it had its most serious advocate in Bernardi, an Italian, who in 1794 incorporated it in his method of "upright swimming." A walking motion of the legs was combined with an alternate forward gathering sweep of the arms. Bernardi in attempting to prove the superiority of his method to all others advanced ridiculous claims for it among which he mentioned that by employing it a swimmer could travel at the rate of three miles per hour. From all early descriptions of treading water nothing can be learned of the employment of the arms but it can be assumed that they were used as an auxiliary means of stroking. One thing is clear, it was used for locomotion rather than for support.

In modern swimming treading water is used as a means of support in an upright position by means of leg strokes alone. The arms are little used and no definite progress is made in any direction. Its value

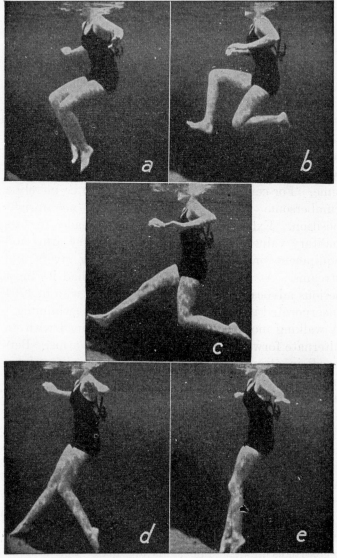

Fig. **39.**—Treading water using single scissors.

lies in making it possible to sustain one's self in deep water by the use of the legs while the hands are occu-pied with removal of clothing, approach and turn of a drowning victim, relief of cramp in the hands and fingers and many other situations which may readily be called to mind. Mastery of treading water is fundamental to good watermanship. Because it is a deep water skill and since it employs leg strokes and adaptations thereof which are used in several styles of swimming, its logical place in the progression is parallel to the acquirement of swimming strokes.

To tread water a slightly forward bent position of the trunk is assumed with the head well-poised on the neck. Both head and neck are held above water. The arms may be extended to the sides horizontally just beneath the surface, to the front with bent elbows, or folded on the chest. The legs are gathered beneath the body in a crouching position from which the stroke is delivered. The legs are stroked in one of three ways; with a single scissors (most commonly), with a breast stroke kick or with a double scissors. All of these strokes are much shortened and delivered at a faster rate than in ordinary swimming. Just enough thrust is delivered to sustain the head above the surface. If a full stroke is delivered it tends to lift the body too high which may result in dropping the face beneath the surface before the next stroke can be taken. The breast stroke kick becomes little more than an outward and downward rotation of the lower legs. The double scissors in its action may be likened to walking a treadmill. The position of the head with the aid of a flexible spine controls the balance.

The learning process for swimmers at this stage of development is not difficult. The upright position is assumed in deep water, while the arms support the learner either by sculling with the hands or using a short gentle breast stroke. Meantime the legs are

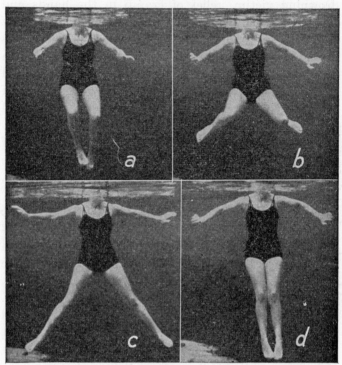

Fig. 40.—Treading water using breast stroke kick.

brought into play and when the power of the thrust and the balance are adjusted the arms may gradually slow their action and eventually stop. Generally, it is a distinct surprise to the novice to note how little effort is required to keep the head above water.

Surface Diving.—While this particular skill is referred to as diving due, no doubt, to its relation to descending to the bottom, it is in reality a swimming skill. Essentially, it is nothing more than a method by which a swimmer moving along the surface of the water in a horizontal position can change his direction swiftly, easily and smoothly so as to swim vertically or obliquely downward.

There are two major methods of doing a surface dive; head foremost from the horizontal position using either a jackknife or a tucked position to angle the body downward or the feet foremost "shooter" which starts from a vertical position. It cannot be said that one is easier or better than another. The ease with which they are accomplished and their efficiency depend upon the physical make-up of the diver and the uses to which they are put. Both methods are presented and both should be mastered.

To do the head foremost surface dive the swimmer lies out along the surface of the water on the belly in swimming position, having some forward momentum. At the start of the dive, if the learner is using the breast stroke, the head is rolled sideward and a breath taken. Immediately, the face is turned down and forward and with a spreading movement of the arms the body is angled downward leaving the legs lying along the surface. If the jackknife is employed, as the body nears the vertical the legs are lifted above the surface sharply in fully extended position until they are in line with the trunk. The arms circle outward meanwhile and as the weight of the lifted legs force the diver downward, the hands are brought forward in front of the chest and then extended downward and forward beyond the head in good diving position.

If the learner finds it difficult to lift the legs to the vertical in fully extended position he may use the tuck with better success. In this form, the diver brings the

Fig. 41.—The jackknife surface dive.

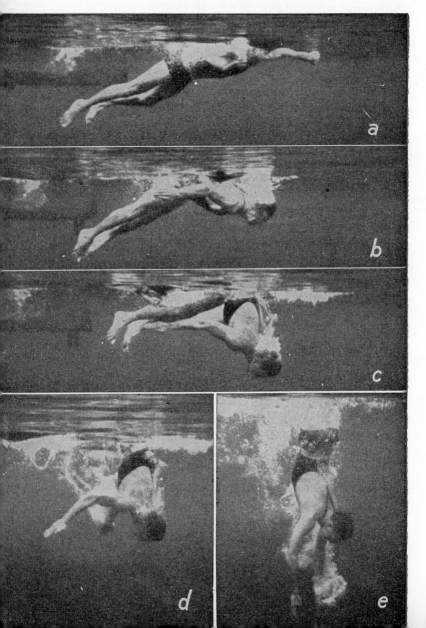

knees toward the chest as his body approaches the
vertical. The position is not unlike that assumed for
a tucked front somersault. As the head swings down

Fig. 42.—Using tuck in surface dive.

to the vertical and as a continuation of the preceding
movement, the legs are extended sharply above the
surface and the diver drives downward in the same
fully extended position as taken in the jackknife dive.
In a surface dive employing either of these forms, it
may be said that anyone should reach a depth two feet
greater than his own length without taking a stroke.
This varies somewhat in individuals depending upon
their buoyancy or lack of it.

There is at least one major safety factor and one
health factor which influence the use of this type of
surface dive. Both must be taken into consideration
in diving to ward off injury and discomfort. The
safety factor is a simple one and may be stated
simply. To avoid injury by striking submerged
objects or the bottom, the hands and arms must be
forward of the head before the diver starts his vertical

descent. The health factor cannot be so easily described and discussed.

Self-taught surface divers in the main present a very peculiar aspect of the form employed which cannot be other than injurious to health in many cases. As they prepare to surface dive, they come to a full stop and allow the legs to drift downward until almost vertical. Then with a surging downward drive of the arms, the head is lifted as far above the surface as possible. A gulp of air is taken and the head is ducked sharply. With something of a struggle, the body makes a hairpin turn and follows the head downward leaving the legs vainly and ineffectually kicking in the air, a mark, by the way, of an amateurish attempt. When the head is ducked sharply forward from its high position the face is brought into violent contact with the surface and a quantity of water is driven into the nostrils with considerable force. This is where much of the discomfort and resultant sinus infection develops and is responsible in no small part for the condemnation of surface diving as a swimming skill, to be avoided if health is to be maintained. This is supplemented by another common practice which is found occurring largely in the early stages of the learning process. In their efforts to get below the surface, learners frequently tuck the chin to the chest as they slide under and in so doing put the nostrils in the best possible position to admit water when every effort should be made to keep it out. In head foremost surface dives the face should always be directed down and forward if the aforementioned condition is to be avoided.

In making a quick surface dive if speed is imperative it is not necessary to change from a crawl or trudgen to the breast stroke before starting the dive. When the swimmer uses a hand-over-hand stroke he should, just before he reaches the spot in which he wishes to dive, leave the forward arm extended beyond the head, take in air as usual, bring the recovering arm forward and extend it parallel to the leading arm. Then the body is angled downward sharply and the arms spread as usual. The dive done in this manner is astonishingly quick and is accomplished with extreme ease.

The feet foremost surface dive is advocated and used by many good swimmers as a safe and very efficient way of going very deep in a speedy and relatively easy manner. It is safer in unknown waters than the head foremost entry, especially when the water is so dark or discolored as to be impenetrable to the gaze. It is, however, necessarily slower because it requires the swimmer to swing to an upright position before the descent can be made.

The feet foremost surface dive is essentially nothing more than a variation of "sounding," a simple method of testing the depth of the water known to everyone who swims. The cry "So deep!" and the sight of a boy or girl pinching the nostrils shut with one hand and extending the other above the head as he or she sinks beneath the surface is a common element in every swimming scene.

To do a surface dive feet foremost, the swimmer first assumes an upright position in the water. Then with quick sharp strokes of arms and legs he lifts the head and shoulders above the surface as high as possible. As he sinks back the legs are brought close together and the toes are pointed to lessen resistance in the downward plunge. The arms are held fully extended along the sides and as the head drops below the surface they are swept out and upward, palms uppermost, in one broad vigorous sweep until they meet fully extended above the head. Often, a swimmer of

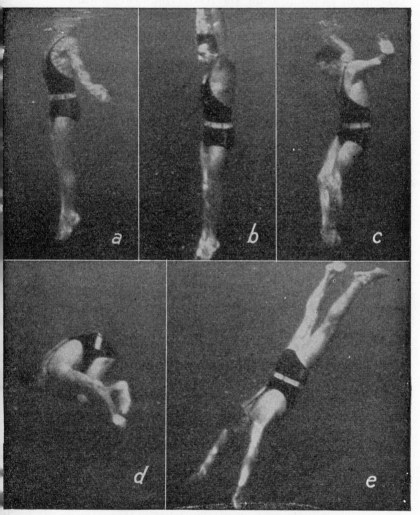

Fig. 43.—Surface dive, feet foremost.

inconsiderable buoyancy will arrive at the bottom in from twelve to fifteen feet of water without further effort. When the momentum achieved in the first downward plunge begins to lessen, the diver has two courses of action open to him depending on what he wishes to do. If he desires to swim horizontally, he folds up, changes his line of progress to the horizontal and swims away. If he wants to go still deeper, he tucks and turns to a head downward position and, having reversed his body position, straightens out and continues downward by swimming.

A surface dive is the graceful way of entering the world that lies beneath the surface of the water. Man cannot hope to achieve the ease and grace of the otter or the loon in stooping from the surface nor can he ever hope to know the underwater world as well as they do because of his breath-holding limitations. He can, however, perfect the art of surface diving as it is modified to suit his physical structure, and learn to slip under water with ease and beauty of action. One of the major exhilarations of all swimming comes with the ability to cleave one's way downward into the cool green depths of a crystal clear lake or lagoon and there to remain for a little while in full enjoyment of a new and different world. It is with reluctance that the skilled diver turns back to the surface after such an experience.

Under-water Swimming.—The desire to learn how to swim under water seems to be a natural inclination of many novices. The wish to explore a new and different world may be the dominant motivating force but the acquirement of it has real and definite value to the all-around swimmer. It can be used to reach bottom in waters of reasonable depth to recover lost

objects or drowned victims.   It may be used to search
the bottom for the same purposes by swimming just
above it.   It has proven its value in a number of
instances on record where men lost overboard from
steamers have had to swim deep to avoid being drawn
into thrashing paddle wheels or churning screws.

There is nothing complex about under-water swimming.   The breast stroke is used almost universally.
For moving rapidly in clear water, the arms are pulled
clear to the sides with hands finishing at the thighs,
completing the pull as the legs close and allowing the
body to glide torpedo-fashion for an appreciable
distance before the next stroke.   Under any condition
in which visibility is poor or obscured a quarter stroke
of the arms is employed so that the head may at all
times be protected by the out-stretched hands from
collision with hidden obstructions.   Under way, the
direction of the swimmer is governed by movements
of the head.   To descend the head is dropped forward
and to ascend it is raised.   A little practice will enable
the swimmer to change his direction or his level at will
and with ease.   (See Fig. 44).

A type of under-water locomotion which has definite
value but is not commonly known or used, is the
combination of breast stroke with the arms and thrust
against the bottom with the feet.   In a crouched position on the bottom, the feet are placed one forward and
the other slightly to the rear in much the same position
that a sprinter takes to start a foot race.   With the
head well down and forward a vigorous shove is given
with the feet and as the body shoots forward, a wide
breast stroke pull of the arms gives added impetus to
the body.   The glide is then taken in torpedo-fashion
a foot or eighteen inches above the bottom; i. e., with

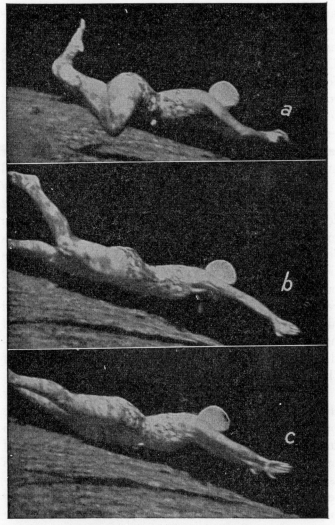

Fig. 44.—Swimming under water.

arms held close to the sides, hands against the thighs and legs closed. As headway diminishes, the legs are again drawn beneath the body and the thrust repeated. Care must be taken to keep the head well down and forward so that contact with the bottom will not be lost. With this combined method of using arms and legs, a course along the bottom can be covered with great rapidity.

The eyes, of course, are kept open in under-water swimming. Even in extremely clear water, vision will be blurred and indistinct, but objects may be readily recognized by their outlines and color. In searching for small objects such as lost eyeglasses or jewelry, an extraordinary practice has been devised which gives for a few minutes practically clear vision. At the bottom with the head raised slightly the hands are cupped above the eyes and a small quantity of air released from the mouth. This air rushing upward along the face is caught and held by the tightly cupped hands to form an air pocket before the eyes. Immediately the bottom is seen with startling clarity and if the object is within range, it is quickly detected.

The human species is limited in its ability to stay under water by its capacity to hold the breath. One breath must suffice for each trip under water and man must always return to the surface for a fresh supply of air. Holding the breath beyond the first few seconds is not a particularly pleasing experience and if prolonged by force of will or accidental circumstance beyond the point at which symptoms of distress are felt, it will become agonizing and even result in loss of consciousness and death. The interval spent under water may be prolonged and distress lessened by suitable preparation and by practice. To prepare to swim under water the swimmer should exhale deeply and inhale shallowly for a period of about a half minute. Just before the plunge is taken the lungs should be inflated to two-thirds capacity. If the lungs are inflated to full capacity, distress will be felt almost at once due to the strain put upon them. A trickling release of air from the nose, if started at the first sign of discomfort, will help to prolong the stay under water by postponing distress.

Deep Swimming.—Staying under water merely for the purpose of demonstrating how long the breath can be held, to what depth the swimmer can descend or what distance can be covered is unwise and dangerous. Descending to extraordinary depths is warranted only if a life is to be saved thereby and no other means for recovering the victim from the bottom are at hand. Even then it is governed by the rescuer's knowledge of his own capacity for such a feat. Anyone who considers himself a swimmer should be able to reach bottom in ten feet of water and swim at that depth a distance of fifteen feet with comparative ease and no distress.

A great deal that is fallacious has been said and written about deep diving. It has been assumed that at any considerable depth the water by its great weight would squeeze the unprotected body in such manner as to cause congestion of the brain and internal organs and even collapse the chest walls. A little reflection will serve to demonstrate that, since the body itself is largely fluid any pressure of the water will instantly be transmitted through all the tissues. In one sense it may be said that the pressure is absorbed. Within three portions of the body, however, there are air spaces which cannot absorb the pressure. The lungs and windpipe constitute one, the sinuses of the head another, and the tiny space back of the ear drum a third. Surrounding the lungs is a bony case composed of ribs, spine and breastbone which while compressible, nevertheless, offers considerable resistance to the pressure of the water. The sinuses of the head are wonderfully protected by the structure of the skull, but, unfortunately, two openings (the nostrils), permit access of water because there is no natural mechanism for closing them. The air space of the middle ear is particularly susceptible to pressure because it is protected only by the thin, elastic membrane of the eardrum. These three areas, then, are the only ones in which the swimmer is really vulnerable to the pressure of the water at extraordinary diving depths.

To understand what happens in deep diving, it would be well to follow in fancy the descent of a hypothetical diver. Assume that he has lung capacity sufficient to remain under water for forty-five seconds. With the initial impetus of his downward plunge plus one or two breast strokes he reaches a depth of ten or twelve feet with little effort and small discomfort. At about fifteen feet he is made uncomfortably aware of distressing pain in the ears. As he goes deeper the pain becomes ever more acute and is accompanied by pains of growing intensity in the eyes, the forehead and the temples. The water seems to take on the consistency of glue, strokes become shorter and progress downward is slower. At twenty-five feet the average good swimmer reaches the limit of his capacity and must turn and make his way upward. Upon reaching the surface once more the acute pain in the ears and over the eyes passes, leaving in its wake a throbbing headache that may not clear up for some hours, and no inclination to repeat the performance. When the diver returns to shore he may be disconcerted to find a thin stream of water pouring from his nostrils. This usually happens some minutes after the dive and may recur intermittently for an hour or more after that. This is a clear indication that the water under pressure has penetrated into the head sinuses during the dive. The possibilities of sinus infection as a result of it are readily apparent.

It is not difficult for the better than average swimmer to overcome these handicaps. To prevent water penetration, all that is necessary is to keep the mouth closed and pinch the nostrils shut with a clip device. (A small spring clothespin serves very well.) A little practice will enable the swimmer to use it without discomfort. The second handicap, pressure on the eardrums, needs a little more detailed explanation. Everyone knows the anatomy of the external ear; the shape of it, the canal which penetrates into the head and the drumhead or tympanum which marks the terminus of the external portion. What lies behind the tympanum is not so well known to many swimmers. Immediately behind the drumhead is the middle ear. It consists of a small chamber (carinu tympani—eardrum) and a canal (the Eustachian tube), which leads down and inward opening into the nasopharynx which is the chamber just beyond the nostrils. Through the Eustachian tube the eardrum is ventilated by air drawn into the nasopharynx. At the upper end of the tube where it adjoins the eardrum there is a constricted portion known as the isthmus. This isthmus is sometimes so constricted that the eardrum is quite cut off from the remainder of the respiratory tract. A partial vacuum is formed in the eardrum and any excess pressure from without tends to press the drumhead inward against parts of the ear which are peculiarly sensitive to pressure.   So, in deep diving the pressure on the drumhead as it increases may cause intolerable pain to the diver.

Fortunately, however, the diver has a ready means for overcoming the condition aforementioned.   As he penetrates to depths at which the pressure begins to cause discomfort, he may swallow several times or blow forcibly with the mouth and nose closed, thereby opening the isthmus and utilizing the air pressure of the remainder of the respiratory tract to equalize the water pressure without.   It is remarkable to note how quickly the discomfort and pain is relieved by this simple action.   As the expert swimmer accustoms himself to deep diving he will find that the pressure in the ears will be equalized automatically as he descends making unnecessary the swallowing or blowing process.

Before the subject is closed, in the interest of safety, it must be stated once more that deep diving is useful in extreme emergencies and is a skill which belongs to expert watermen.   The majority of swimmers should confine their diving activities to depths not greater than 15 feet.

Useful Variations of Strokes

There are literally hundreds of variations of strokes and styles of swimming ranging from the many and ingenious movements used by unskilled swimmers to compensate for lack of rhythm and wasted energies, to the minute yet carefully calculated departures from standard strokes employed by competitive swimmers to increase speed.   There are, also many combinations of movements and variations of position which may be

classed under the general head of "stunts." Some
variations are made quite unconsciously and to no
purpose, others are studied deviations from the usual
methods with a limited objective in view. Purpose-
less variation has already been dealt with in the discussion on "Learning How to Swim," and "Styles of
Swimming." The seemingly endless variety of stunts
in swimming may be classified as useful since they are
a great factor in the development of all-around swimming ability but since their number is so great, they
are not included here.

A few variations of accepted styles of swimming
appear so frequently especially among those who are
self-taught, that they seem worthy of attention and
description. While they are not standard they have
such a degree of efficiency and are so commonly used
by many swimmers, they must be recognized.

Variation of Breast Stroke.—The first of these is a
variation of the breast stroke which differs from the
normal only in the position of the body. In this manner of swimming, the body is angled down and backward until the feet may be as much as three feet below
the surface. Obviously, the purpose of it is to keep
the face above water at all times without the necessity
of lifting the head by muscular action. Progress is
much slower to be sure but that it is a very comfortable
way of swimming cannot be denied. For group swimming in leisurely fashion it becomes the most sociable
of all swimming styles since the swimmer can see, hear
and talk without interruption. It is most commonly
used by swimmers of continental Europe, where group
swimming is something more than a mere trial of speed.

Butterfly Breast Stroke.—Into competitive swimming has come comparatively recently a variation of

the breast stroke known as the "butterfly." Essentially it is a double overarm stroke in which both arms pull down and backward through the water and recover

Fig. 45.—Butterfly.

to starting position over the surface simultaneously. In the arm position it is nothing more nor less than a crawl stroke in which the arms stroke and recover together rather than alternately. The leg stroke while somewhat narrowed remains essentially the same as in the regular breast stroke. The timing of legs and arms may be alternate, with a glide at the completion of each stroke or practically simultaneous with little or no gliding interval between strokes.

As the stroke has developed it appears to require more than the usual amount of flexibility in the shoulder-joint and strength. In its present state its requirements seem to be too exacting to permit its use over any but distances up to two hundred and twenty yards but as the true crawl was developed out of a crude method of whacking away at the water, so this stroke too may be the forerunner of an improved style of swimming of great usefulness. At present, however, it appears to be simply a method of gaining a little more speed in breast stroke competition.

Inverted Side Stroke.—It is interesting to note that among untutored swimmers who swim a side stroke, approximately three out of ten reverse the usual order of things in the scissors stroke of the legs; that is, the top leg reaches to the rear while the under leg is extended forward to take the scissors position. The arms stroke in orthodox fashion. The scissors is much wider and delivered with more vigor than it is in the usual position. While resistance in the negative portion of the stroke is greater and progress slower, it has measurably more power in the thrust. A swimmer equipped with this stroke is usually much better fitted to learn life saving than one who swims the side stroke in orthodox fashion because the leg position of the stroke is more powerful and no change is necessary in any of the carries with the exception of that employed to assist a tired swimmer. (See Fig. 46).

Shallow Arm Pull.—A variation of the arm portion of the side stroke is coming more and more into general use among swimmers. The shallow arm pull, so-called, has been used extensively for many years in life saving carries so, perhaps, its application to the regular side stroke is but an adaptation of what has been learned in life saving.

Briefly, the shallow arm pull is nothing but a curving sweep or pull of the lower or forward arm from its extended position beyond the head, to a position beneath the body about six to eight inches under the surface. It has much to recommend it for use in the side stroke, since it can be effectively co-ordinated with the remainder of the stroke and has less tendency to upset the longitudinal balance of the body in stroke.

Fig. 46.—Inverted side stroke.

Because of its effectiveness, it would not be surprising to
see this adaptation come into general use in place of the
vertical pull of the lower arm in side stroke swimming.

Double Trudgen.—Many persons who swim the
trudgen use a variation of the stroke quite naturally

which has some elements of value.   Instead of using a scissors of the legs on one side only and allowing the legs to trail through the remainder of the stroke, a second leg stroke is added with the pull of the other arm.   In effect, it is a scissors of the legs delivered first to one side co-ordinating with the arm pull on that side and then to the other side in conjunction with the pull of the other arm.   The double trudgen stroke may be used very effectively by swimmers whose legs tend to sink in the trailing position employed in the trudgen.   By adding the extra leg scissors the horizontal position can be maintained.

Legless Crawl.—Another variation of a style of swimming the usefulness of which seems to warrant its inclusion under this head, is the so-called "legless crawl."   Briefly, it is nothing more than the complete elimination of the leg portion of the crawl.   Its use is recommended to swimmers who have so much buoyancy in the legs that they are unable to lower the feet far enough beneath the surface to get real drive in the flutter kick.   For swimmers of this physical type it is recommended that the legs and feet be carried fully extended and close together while the arms employ the usual crawl stroking movement. Complete extension of the feet should be attained by extension exercises and practice until the front of the feet can be aligned with the extended legs without discomfort.

Straight Arm Recovery in the Crawl Strokes.—In competitive swimming a variation in the recovery of the arms in the crawl has been used for some years. One school of swimming thought in Europe has held that the straight arm recovery is more efficient than the high elbow recovery generally used and many of the better competitive swimmers in European countries, notably Jean Taris of France and Stephen Barany of Hungary, have excelled in its use to a point

Fig. 47.—Straight arm recovery in back crawl.

where they were able to set world standards at one hundred and four hundred meters, marks that later were bettered. In this country the straight arm recovery has been little used in free style swimming but in the back crawl it is coming into use extensively for competitive purposes. Its foremost exponent, Adolph Kiefer of Chicago, has set numerous records at varying distances using the straight arm recovery.

The recovery of the arm is made with a straight arm sweep in which the arm swings from the shoulder describing an arc just above the surface to the point of entry for the next stroke. It is not unlike the action employed in rowing where the oar is swung back to position to take a stroke. Wherein lies its effectiveness is difficult to determine. The most reasonable explanation thus far offered seems to be that the sweep of the recovering arm increases the application of power in the stroke of the opposite arm applied through the axis of the shoulder. This may have some basis in fact. Other factors must be considered, however, particularly the physical structure of its exponents and the strength needed to use it effectively.

No opinion can be offered on the value of the straight arm recovery to anything but competitive swimming until it is proved by extensive use that average swimmers of average buoyancy and strength can employ it efficiently and sustain the action over much longer distances than those swum competitively.

Elementary Turn.—Much of the swimming practice in the United States takes place in pools or tanks either indoors at all seasons of the year or in open air pools during the summer. These artificially formed bathing places are limited in area and are generally rectangular in shape. Swimming practice therefore is limited to confined or closed courses beginning at one side or end and finishing at the other. As the standard pool is only twenty-five yards long, the possibility of swimming continuously for any great distance without changing stroke is automatically made impossible. To enable the practicing swimmer to cover constantly increasing distances in closed courses with a minimum loss of time and energy at the ends of the course, methods of turning have been devised. The art of turning swiftly and efficiently has reached its acme among competitive swimmers where it has been definitely proved that a good sprint swimmer can actually swim faster in a closed course than he can in

Fig. 48.—Elementary turn.

open water.   The purpose of the simple turn about to
be described is, however, not to gain speed but to
equip every novice and practicing swimmer with a
means of stopping the stroke, changing direction and
getting started again with some degree of ease.

In principle all turns are basically alike.   The
swimmer reaches the vertical face of the side or end
of the pool in fully extended swimming position,
touches or grasps the wall itself or the projecting edge
of the over-flow trough, pulls the knees toward the
chin until the body is tucked into a compact knot,
rotates or twists in that position to the desired swimming position (back, side or front), places both feet
firmly against the wall, shoves off and straightens the
body, and slides into swimming position for the
return journey over the same course.   For the practicing swimmer a secure grasp on the lip of the over-
flow trough with one or, in the case of the breast
stroke, two hands, a pull in and a full breath taken
before shoving off makes a good turn more certain
albeit less rapid.   In the elementary back stroke, the
inverted breast stroke and the back crawl, either one
or both arms are extended beyond the head as the
swimmer nears the wall.   The extended hand seizes
the edge with a hooked grasp, the swimmer rolls
toward the grasping hand, pulls the knees up simultaneously and seizes the edge with the other hand.
When the swimmer has both feet securely placed against
the wall and is facing the wall squarely, a breath is
taken and the push-off made.   In both side strokes
the top arm reaches forward and grasps the edge
and the turn is made on the side and away from
the holding hand.   In all hand-over-hand strokes
(trudgen, trudgen-crawl and crawl), the grasp is

taken with the leading hand, the tuck and the turn to the front position are made simultaneously and the head lifted and breath taken before the grasp is released. The push-off in the front position is made with both arms extended in front of the head. The turn in the breast stroke differs from that in the hand-over-hand strokes only in one thing; the grasp is taken with both hands.

The ability to turn easily in a closed course is important to the learning swimmer of any degree of ability beyond the beginner level. If the tank swimmer is ever to be anything more than a spurt swimmer limited to the width or the length of the tank in a single effort, he must learn to turn well. Therefore, practice on the simple turns must parallel stroke development. Good practice can be had even by the most expert swimmers by swimming widths of narrow pools and turning almost continuously for a period of some minutes. Swimming ten widths of a pool thirty feet wide will afford practice for the average swimmer on nine turns within a period of less than two minutes. It has been said that tank swimming is developing a large portion of the swimming public in this country into spurt swimmers; that a twenty or twenty-five yard limit is imposed by habit upon the swimmer of this type and that when he faces open water conditions in which greater effort is needed to cover longer distances, he is lost. This condition is quite probably due more to the slavish imitation of competitive sprint swimmers by novices equipped with only half-mastered speed strokes than anything else but it is undoubtedly true that inability to swim continuously in confined areas due to lack of turning ability, has contributed to it.

CHAPTER VI

DIVING

The word "dive" means to descend beneath the surface of the water by almost any means; witness the fact that submarines, seekers after pearls and men who descend to the bottom in protective suits are said to "dive" even though they may have submerged by settling, have been pulled down by a weight or have slid down a descending line. To swimmers, however, the term "dive" means mainly to jump or to plunge head foremost beneath the surface from an elevation. The loose terminology employed in this respect has been productive of some confusion in the past and is still somewhat bothersome because of the many interpretations of the term "dive." Thus, it is frequently stated that a person does a "surface dive" even though the act itself is distinctly a swimming skill. A swimmer remarks that he has just dived to a depth of 25 feet when he is quite aware of the fact that he *swam* downward most of the distance. A beginner learns to dive head foremost and any feet foremost entry into the water is a jump or leap to him but a fancy diver performing a complicated acrobatic maneuver in the air and entering the water in an erect position is said to have done a foot dive. Ralph Thomas, noting this confusion, advocated a change in terminology to clarify matters. He urged the adoption of the term "springing" to apply to any means of entering the water from an elevation whether

it be foot or head foremost, high or low, plain or fancy.
His proposal, however, had no success among English
speaking people as by this time the word "dive" had
been so long employed that no change was possible,
despite the undoubted soundness of his proposition.
The swimming world, therefore, will continue to use
the term "dive" to describe a variety of submersions
and place its own interpretation on the procedure
involved and no great difficulty will result except for
those who attempt classification.

Prehistory of Diving.—It is idle to speculate upon
the prehistory of diving. The man who first dared to
strike out and swim was followed closely one can be
sure, by the man who first leaped of his own volition
into deep water. Of only one phase of the early
development of diving can it be said with any degree
of certainty that one thing preceded another in diving
development. It is more than probable that leaping
feet foremost preceded head foremost entry into the
water. Some primitive peoples who are otherwise
expert in swimming enter the water feet foremost by
habit and preferance even to this day.

What courage it must have taken the first swimmer
to make that initial "header." Did he experience the
qualms that beset everyone in a first plunge, the sinking
sensation at the pit of the stomach, the fear of going too
deep, too flat? And after that first ringing thwack as
he struck the water on his belly, how long did it take to
summon enough courage to try it again? Questions
that cannot be answered, of course, but from our own
experience the answers can be guessed.

Brief History of Diving.—In the literature of early
times which has been preserved, there are frequent
references to the act of plunging into the water but not

the method. Olaus Magnus in a book written by him in 1555 depicts in a woodcut what is probably the first visible evidence of a manner of diving in all swimming literature. There are many subsequent references to diving in many books on swimming but until the beginning of the nineteenth century the allusions are to the plain method of entering the water head or feet foremost for the purpose of swimming. Then there begins to appear references to other motivations and other methods of diving. The well-divers of India were described and their ability to leap from a height of as much as eighty feet into a tank, without injury was a marvel to the people of that time. Other high divers or rather jumpers (for they were accustomed to enter the water feet foremost) came along from time to time to give exhibitions and to astound the populace with their prowess. "One Samuel Scott, an American diver who contrived accidentally to hang himself on Waterloo Bridge in 1841 . . . generally went down head foremost" according to Thomas. The motivation back of this suddenly aroused interest in high diving was, to be sure, sensationalism but it marked a step in the development of another skill related to aquatics.

Origin of Acrobatic Diving.—At about the turn of the 17th century (1800) diving in another form was given a new impetus. In Germany and in Sweden formal gymnastics as a means of physical exercise for city and town dwellers came into vogue and began to be exceedingly popular. Almost at once the apparatus used in the gymnasium was transferred to the swimming beach in the summer months where exercise was taken out-of-doors. The springboard, the flying rings and the trapeze were soon adapted to the new conditions. High platforms were erected and soon gymnastics over the water were in full swing. The transition was made easily, simply by substituting the water as a landing cushion for the less yielding gymnasium mat.

This was the beginning in Europe at any rate of fancy diving which was and still is aerial acrobatics over the water. As this phase of diving developed the rings and trapeze were used less and less and the springboard and platform more and more and with the advent of fancy and high diving competition the rings and trapeze were completely discarded.

In other times and in other places certain people developed forms of diving with different motivation and purpose. Early visitors to Hawaii, notably Lady Brassey, remarked the ability of some Hawaiians to leap, dive and somersault from considerable heights. An occasional pool of water, generally at the foot of a waterfall, surrounded by precipitous walls provided the means and the sporting attitude of a joyous and happy people to whom physical excellence was a quality to be admired, provided the motivation. In India the means and motive of well-jumping were quite different. There certain native princes caused tanks to be built surrounded by galleries and the divers performed for the amusement of royalty. This places them in the category of mountebanks but their feats are no less noteworthy because of it.

Value of Diving.—It is not necessary for all swimmers to become high divers or aerial gymnasts but there are certain plain forms of diving which are complementary to swimming and have definite use. Thus, anyone who learns to swim should parallel his development of swimming skills with progressive training in diving. Any swimmer should be able to

enter the water head or feet foremost from solid platform, boat or springboard. He should develop the
ability to plunge shallowly or deeply, to control the
depth of his dive and to level off into swimming position with ease. For mere utility, diving ability
enables the swimmer to enter the water from any point
above the surface, to plunge deeply if he desires to
reach the bottom without waste of time or energy and,
in plain headers, to assume a swimming position on the
surface with ease and facility.

Apart from the more obvious uses of diving there are
a whole series of values in the practice of diving which
are less apparent because they cannot be classified as
useful. These related values are, however, important
to the swimmer and are developed in exact proportion
to the progress made.

The development of courage in the individual is, perhaps, the most fundamental of values in diving. To
fling one's self headlong into the water in a first dive
takes real courage as anyone can testify and to increase
the height or vary the skill calls for proportionately
greater display of "nerve." It is evident that the
habit and continued practice of "getting up nerve" to
try diving skills increases courage which is only another
way of saying "confidence in one's self."

The practice of diving is a very excellent way of
making up for a deficiency which is common to many
persons, namely, the lack of kinesthetic sense. Kines-
thesia is simply a perception or awareness of muscular
movements; it is the feeling of knowing just what
arms, legs and body are doing when they are being
moved. To cite an example, a class in a gymnasium
is ordered to raise arms sideward to shoulder level. It
is surprising to note the number of individuals who

raise the arms to a point either above or below the level indicated without being aware of the deviation unless they deliberately look at them. They display only the most elementary development of this kinesthetic sense but if they are made to correct and repeat the movement and position it takes little time to bring it under control. Diving requires much greater development of this sense perception than elementary arm exercises because all of the parts are involved and must be controlled in the brief interval of flight from the board or platform to the water. Increasing grace and agility are developed as a result of such practice.

The worth of diving as an exercise must not be discounted. The stretching of the body, the arm-swinging movements, the play of muscles in maintaining balance and the springing of the legs are all factors which help to build musculature, agility and vitality in the individual.

Fundamentals of Diving.—There are some factors which are common to all diving skills. Some of them are related to safety and others to comfort but all are vitally concerned in making of diving a safe and pleasant experience. Foremost in point of safety must be the assurance that the water is deep enough for the type of dive attempted. The list of those who have dashed against the bottom with injury or death as a result is a long one. It must be made certain that there are no submerged or floating obstructions which might cause injury or worse, if struck. The elevation from which the diver takes off must afford secure footing and be strong enough to hold against the thrust that is made against it. Slippery docks and diving boards, insecure diving platforms and badly

pitched springboards have been the cause of many
water accidents. The diver must always leap or
spring far enough away from his take-off point to clear
every part of its structure. This is particularly true
in fancy diving as in some categories of dives the
direction of the body is toward the board.

It is doubtful if anyone ever advanced very far in
diving without experiencing the discomfort of a stinging slap on the back or front on the surface of the
water. The discomfort of this experience can be
minimized, however, by controlling the position in
the air and by acquirement of the ability to "fold up"
just before hitting the surface if the dive has gone
out of control. The head is the major controlling
factor in diving and the arms and the body to a lesser
extent. The head is a heavy and compact mass of
bone and tissue which, if it deviates from the line of
flight in the dive, tends to travel faster than the rest
of the body, thereby pivoting the diver to another
position. To make this clear a few examples may be
cited. A beginning diver crouches on a low take-off
point. In his anxiety to keep from landing flat he
drops his chin to his chest and falls forward. The
head swings down and inward and he lands on his
back. A diver leaves a springboard for a plain
header. He throws his head backward away from
his line of flight and immediately causes his body to
swing as far away in the opposite direction and as a
result he lands flat on the front. On one occasion a
girl who was quite a good diver elected to try a very
high dive. Having had no experience in high diving
she leaped from the platform and headed directly
for the water. Halfway down the momentum of
her head turned her completely over in a front somer-

sault and she landed, fortunately, feet foremost in the water. Control of the head lies in the muscles of the neck and the diver must develop the ability to change the position of the head at will to govern the angle of the dive.

The art of saving one's self from the possibility of discomfort and injury even though the dive has gone hopelessly out of control is not easily learned. In principle it is nothing more than bringing the knees to the chin, tucking the head well in and landing in a compact knot. Flat surfaces hitting the water receive the full force of the impact but a curved surface has the faculty of taking up the shock and minimizing it. In actuality, it takes some practice to determine just when a dive is hopelessly lost and to "tuck up" quickly from the open position.

Entry into the water is made also with due regard for the comfort and safety of the diver. In all head foremost dives the arms are extended beyond the head and in the line of flight for two reasons, first to open a hole for the head to enter thereby avoiding direct impact upon the skull and second, to avoid injury to the head by contact with the bottom if the dive is unexpectedly deep. This position is held until the diver actually touches bottom or turns and starts upward. There is a tendency among uninstructed divers to pull the arms back under the body as soon as the fingertips touch the water with the result that the full impact is taken on the head or face. The legs must be held fully extended on the entry into the water if stinging slaps on thighs and calves are to be avoided.

For any height greater than 10 feet, the entry into the water for head foremost dives should always be made with clenched fists. Open hands, no matter how rigidly extended, may be deflected by impact with the water. The elbows may be bent or the arms thrown out of line and the full shock of the contact taken directly on the head. From considerable heights, this deflection may cause the shoulder to be wrenched severely. Moreover, the area of two clenched fists closely aligned will serve to punch a larger hole in the surface for admission of the head. The hands are clenched just before they touch the water, so they do not impair the form displayed, noticeably.

Entry in feet foremost dives is made with the body fully extended, legs closed and the arms close to the sides. In this type of entry a factor is involved which is the cause of a great deal of discomfort among those who dive. As the head slides under water the force of the downward rush tends to force water into the open nostrils. If it stopped there it would not be so distressing but the pressure frequently drives the water into the head sinuses with subsequent irritation and possible infection. The beginning diver solves the problem very nicely by holding the nostrils shut between thumb and finger. Beyond the beginner level, however, no diver likes to be bothered with a practice so amateurish in nature and fortunately it is not necessary. When the face reaches the water, the diver exhales a stream of air from the nostrils which, as long as it continues will not allow water to enter. At first, this must be done with conscious effort but in a surprisingly short time the action will become largely automatic.

Once completely under water a dive is finished. From then on it is a matter of checking the downward drive, changing position and returning to the surface. In feet foremost entry if the water is less than seven or eight feet deep, the diver lands on the toes on the bottom, lets the knees sag to take up possible shock and then pushes off to the surface. In water of greater depth the arms and legs are spread after the body is under water and then the diver swims upward to the surface. The diver returns to the surface from plain headers of the plunging or shallow variety simply by turning the fingertips upward and lifting the head. In deeper dives swimming movements are used to aid in regaining the surface. Among fancy divers, especially in the average swimming pool, the endeavor to get good position and clean entry into the water often results in driving the diver all the way to the bottom even in "headers." That this is not serious or particularly dangerous to the good diver is indicated by the fact that when the hands touch bottom the body is brought into a tucked position, the feet placed on the bottom and the return journey to the surface aided by a push-off.

Plain Diving

Learning How to Dive.—Beginning swimmers need little instruction for leaping feet foremost into the water. If standing on the take-off they simply leap from both feet exactly as they would in jumping on land, and if they choose to run, usually take off from one foot. In water of moderate depth, the toes touch the bottom and the jumper falls forward on the surface in swimming position. In deep water he comes up and levels off as previously described.

When a person starts to learn how to dive head foremost, the process of learning is not quite so simple.

A learning progression is given therefore to make plain diving easy and not quite so painful as the rough and ready methods in general use.   In principle it seeks

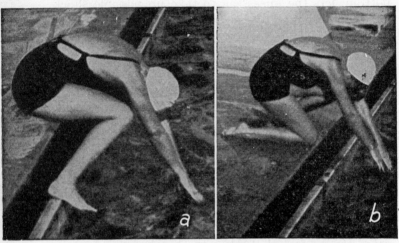

Fig. 49A.—Beginner diving.   First step.
Fig. 49B.—Beginner diving.   Second step.

to start the learner as near water-level as possible, give him the correct angle of entry and make it impossible to bring the legs forward.

The first header taken by a beginner is but a step beyond the push-off and glide.   In water of mid-thigh depth, the learner extends the arms forward, tucks the face between the upper arms, crouches, leans outward until off-balance then falls forward.   As the balance is lost, a little push is given with the feet against the bottom and the diver's head and arms enter the water with the body and legs following.   In appearance, the curve of the body slipping under water is not unlike that of a porpoise in the act of diving.   A little way under water the diver turns the hands and head upward and slides out to a gliding

Fig. 49C,D,E.—Beginner diving. Third step.

position on the surface. A few of these dives accomplished successfully and the novice is ready to begin diving from an elevation.

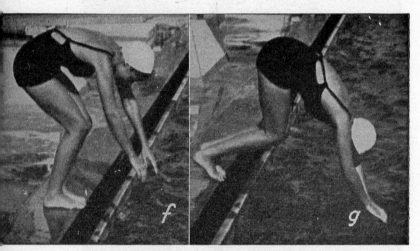

Fig. 49F,G.—Beginner diving. Fourth step.

A point is selected from which to start a few inches above the surface beneath which the water is not less than shoulder deep. This may be the edge of a low dock, a float or the edge of a swimming pool. The diver sits on the edge with the heels in the overflow trough if diving in a pool, on a rung of a ladder or a cleat, if elsewhere. The arms are extended forward and downward pointing to a spot on the surface about three feet away. The palms are turned down, the thumbs locked and the head tucked in between the arms. The cheeks rest against the biceps and the novice looks forward *under* the fingertips. The knees are spread. In this first dive no attempt is made to spring. The body is rocked forward between the knees and the diver, leaving the feet behind, simply slides head foremost into the water, much as a turtle slips off a log. When this can be accomplished with ease, the learner is ready for the next steps.

The advance through the next few steps can be made very rapidly; kneeling on one knee with the other foot on the edge, crouching with one foot on the edge and the other a few inches back, standing with knees slightly bent with one foot back of the other, and standing with both feet parallel and slightly apart. Dives from all of these positions can be taken in rapid succession and practiced until they are done easily. Very little spring is taken and the head must not be lifted or the body straightened until the head and shoulders are under water. These are all novice dives and are little more than falling head foremost into the water. Now real diving begins.

Co-ordinated Standing Front Header.—The standing plain header is in reality only a standing broad jump landing head foremost; that is, the act of springing up and out over the water with vigor is a counterpart of the broad jump in grip of the feet on the take-off, swing and crouch of the start, lift of arms and shoulders and spring of legs and feet. The only difference lies in the landing position.

A standing front header is done in the following manner: The diver stands at the edge of the take-off with feet together and toes gripping the edge. The body is erect and the arms are extended forward at shoulder height. To start the dive, the arms are swung down and backward and the knees slightly bent. As the arms near the end of the back swing the body starts to lean forward. Immediately the arms are drawn forward (not lifted) the hands shoot through under the armpits and the arms are extended

forward again. The knees straighten and the legs
are sprung away from the take-off by lifting sharply
from the heels to the toes. The diver follows the
hands out and down into the water. In the air, the
legs are held close together and fully extended with
the toes pointed. The face is tucked between the
arms either during the flight or just before entering
the water. (See Fig. 50).

Co-ordinated Running Front Header.—Running
front headers from a firm take-off differ from standing
front dives only in the impetus given the diver by the
running approach. The momentum developed carries
the diver farther away from the take-off point. The
run may be long or short, easy or vigorous but in any
case should be free and natural. The take-off may be
made from one or both feet. If it is made from one
foot, the action is again very similar to a running broad
jump, done head foremost. The body is carried well
forward, the last step launches the diver from the edge
of the take-off and immediately the jumping leg is
brought up to a position beside the other leg. If the
take-off is made from both feet, a jump is substituted
for the last step, the diver lands on the balls of the feet
just back of the edge and launches the dive with a
sharp lift from the toes. In taking off from either
one or both feet, it is important that the motion of
the arms be so timed that both arms are swinging forward pendulum fashion as the diver leaves the take-off
point. (See Fig. 51).

Springboard Diving.—Spring (or springing) boards
were first employed by divers as a means of increasing
the range of a dive and prolonging the interval of flight
through the air. Using the lift of a springing board,

the diver can soar a little higher into the air and, if he wishes, dive in a longer arc by this auxiliary means.

The difference in taking off from a springboard as compared to that from a firm deck is at once apparent to the learner. From the dock or float the lift and spring of the dive was achieved wholly by muscular action from an unyielding base. On the springboard, the learner is conscious of a flexing, vibrating instrument which, if used correctly, will contribute a lifting force to his diving efforts. In standing headers and footers the additional lift is readily apparent but it is, of course, greater in running dives.

When the beginning diver has mastered the standing front header from a firm base he is ready to try the springboard. Taking his stance at the end of the board in exactly the same manner as he did on the dock, the arms are swung down and back, then forward as the diver leans outward. On the down swing of the arms, the board will bend downward and on the swing forward it will rise beneath the diver's feet and add its lift to the dive. If the novice has leaned too far outward in his eagerness to get to the water the board will lift feet and legs sharply and turn the diver over on his flight to the water. If the body is held well-poised over the feet and is only slightly off-balance forward, the board will lift the whole weight and project it upward and out far enough to clear the board.

Running Front Header from the Springboard.—A front header taken with a run from a springboard is, without doubt, the acme of plain diving experience. The appreciable interval of soaring flight after lifting from the board is akin to flying and for a fraction of time the diver is pleasantly aware of his release from the pull of gravity which must inevitably bring him back to the water.

To get a maximum of lift from the board, it must bend under the weight of the diver and lift beneath his feet on the recoil to hurl him up and outward. It is axiomatic in diving that "one can get out of the board only as much as he puts into it." This means merely that the deeper the bend of the board, the greater will be the lift. The approach, that is, the action of the diver on the board, determines the height and control of the dive.

The Approach.—To start the approach the diver stands at the extreme "inboard" end of the spring-board erect and well-poised, arms hanging naturally at the sides. Stepping off, he starts his run along the board in evenly spaced strides of medium length. The arms may start swinging simultaneously at any time in the run. One full stride back of the outboard end the diver leaps from one foot and lands on the toes of both feet just back of the leading edge. This jump, known as the hurdle, should be high and vigorous and the arms must be so timed that they are swinging forward with the leap. The action is exactly the same as it would be in leaping over a low fence. The diver lands on the balls of the feet with the chest directly above the toes, the arms carried slightly forward, and circling outward. With the muscles of the legs tensed, the weight of the diver bends the board downward. As it rebounds the arms swing forward and upward, the legs and feet are extended sharply and the diver leaves the board. In the air, the arms continue their swing and are extended to the sides horizontally in the "swan" position while the back is arched. In flight the head describes a short arc and the feet and legs a long one more swiftly, bringing the body to a position just beyond the horizontal at the top of the dive; that is, with the feet a

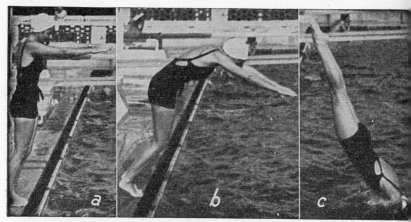

Fig. 50.—Co-ordinated standing front header.

little higher than the head. Thence, the diver drops back to the water with the head falling faster than the legs which brings the body into correct alignment for entry into the water. Just before the diver enters the water, the fully extended arms are brought forward of the head and the face tucked between the biceps.

Learning the Approach.—For some persons the process of learning how to do a running front header from a diving board is short; for others, it is long, involved and sometimes discouraging, yet its achievement is possible by almost any swimmer. Its mastery involves much practice with attention concentrated on learning and controlling one thing at a time. Thus, the novice enters upon a series of learning steps for the approach. First, he stands on the end of the board and with arms circling, bounds up and down. In the

beginning these bounds are little more than lifts onto
the toes but gradually as the balance is caught and
maintained they lift higher and higher with the whip

of the board until the diver may be springing straight
up as high as two or three feet in a series of ten or more
leaps.   This is good practice to offset the tendency to
leave the board before it lifts and to lean too far outward at the beginning of the dive.   The approach
itself may begin with a jump to the end of the board
and a dive and continue successively with one step, a
hurdle and dive; two steps, hurdle and dive; and so
on until the whole board is being used.   Meantime,
the swinging arms and lifting shoulders are being
fitted into the run to make of the whole approach a
smoothly co-ordinated and effective preparation for
the dive.   (See Fig. 52).

Form in the Air.—Good form in the air is desired by
everyone who dives.   The long clean unbroken line
of a stretched body in flight through the air is at once
pleasing to the diver and to those who may be watching.   The head in line with the spine, the arch in the

back, the closely aligned legs and feet and the pointed toes must all be concentrated upon separately by the learning diver. The tendency to let the knees hinge

Fig. 51.—Co-ordinated running front header, taking off from one foot.

or the feet to fly apart must be steadily resisted and finally overcome, even if mechanical means have to be resorted to. It is a common practice in diving instruction to have the diver go back to standing front dives and hold a piece of cardboard between the ankles as a means of concentrating upon holding the legs and feet together.

For perfect safety in running front headers from a springboard only two things have to be kept in mind. First, the running approach should be free and vigorous to secure momentum enough to carry the diver away from the end of the board, no matter how strenuously he strives for height. Second, the entry into the water should not be made with the back extremely arched. If the diver overthrows in this position the spine may be painfully wrenched. The entry should be made with the back flat or only slightly arched in its upper portion.

The learning process for plain diving should begin, of course, at low elevations and only gradually work up to higher take-off levels. The standard low diving

board is erected one meter from the surface of the water and this is a good height for beginning springboard diving. The highest point for the erection of springboards is three meters for competitive diving and this should mark the limit of springboard diving for all swimmers, as nothing is to be gained above that level. In competitive diving from platforms, levels of five and ten meters are arbitrarily set. The lower of these two is a very good limit for average diving for anyone except the most skilled of fancy and high divers. It is doubtful if children should ever dive head foremost from any level greater than ten feet because of the possible bad effects of the impact on thin-walled skulls.

All of the diving skill necessary as a complementary part of swimming is contained in the foregoing pages on plain diving. These skills once mastered give the swimmer adequate means for entering the water at any angle and from any reasonable height. It is

Fig. 52.—The approach.

doubtful, however, if any but a very few will consider this the end of their diving progress. Diving is much too fascinating a part of aquatics to the average swimmer to be confined to its plain forms.

Leaping from a Height Feet Foremost.—There may come a time in the experience of any swimmer when he will find it necessary to jump from a considerable height into the water. Situations such as leaping from a bridge to the aid of a drowning person or saving one's own life by jumping from the deck of a sinking ship and many others may be visualized easily. It would appear then that anyone who calls himself a swimmer should be somewhat skilled in making a leap of this kind, if he is to avoid injury at a time when this skill is needed.

Over water of suitable depth, the learner should start his practice at a height of no more than five meters. With a little spring the diver leaves his take-off and with elbows in and knees drawn upward toward the body and spread slightly assumes a half-sitting position in the air. The trunk is erect but the head is carried somewhat forward. In this position he drops downward maintaining his balance by quick lunging movements of the head and arms. A few feet above the surface, the legs are extended sharply and held tightly pressed together while the arms are shot above the head. The head is thrown back and in this position the diver enters the water.

As the diver increases his height five or ten feet at a time, the jump will be increasingly hard to control. The tendency to lean outward in the course of the jump must be stoutly resisted if the body is not to be over balanced forward. The diver should note his position in the jump by looking down the nose and direct his gaze at the water, between the spread knees.

For practice and the development of skill in high leaping it is not necessary to go above a height of twenty feet.

Fancy Diving

There is a vast difference in skill between that of the child engaged in leaping from the float and turning about in the air to land in the water facing his take-off point, and the highly trained competitive diver doing a two-and-a-half somersault forward from a high springboard, yet in essence they are both indulging in fancy diving regardless of the degree of difficulty. Any purposeful variation of position or direction in flight, so long as it is not grotesque, can be classified as a fancy dive.

A good fancy diver is the cynosure of all eyes. The admiration and, occasionally, envy of spectators and other swimmers is evident whenever he performs. To some who would learn to dive as he does, his somersaulting, twisting and diving seem absurdly easy while to others emulation of his feats seems hopelessly beyond them. A little reflection will serve to bring understanding of his prowess as a diver. First, it is known that he started his diving practice on the same general level that all swimmers must in learning how to get into the water head or feet foremost. Mastery of plain diving had to precede the fancy forms and the learning process for developing the combinations of positions and directions was a long and often tedious one. Simple fancy dives had to precede more complex forms and endless attention had to be paid to refining every part of each dive. Co-ordination and timing were not established in a mere half dozen diving attempts.

Diving Sense.—Some persons are gifted with what can be called "diving sense." That is, they seem to have a general awareness of every position taken and every move made. For these few fortunate individuals progress beyond the plain diving level is generally very rapid. At the other end of the scale are the few who completely lack kinesthetic sense. They are the ones who hurl themselves blindly from the dock or board with no idea of where they are going, what they are doing or how they will hit the water. The vast majority of learners in diving occupy a position somewhere about midway between these two extremes. Their progress will be in exact proportion to the amount of time and application they give to practice.

Fancy diving is limited to no particular type of physique. Excessively stout persons and those who have heavy legs and light bodies will not go very far in fancy diving. As a rule, tall and rangy persons do better with open dives and twists, while the shorter more compact individuals make better somersaulters, especially on low springboards. This condition does not always hold true, however. Tall slender men and women are seen occasionally who tuck into the tightest of somersaults and occasionally a tall heavy individual appears on the swimming scene who dives exceedingly well. The average woman does not do multiple somersault dives well because they require trunk musculature which is not normal for her sex. It is doubtful if effort should be made to develop the muscles involved in this type of diving. By preference, it is advisable for her to confine her efforts to other forms to which her physical structure is better adapted.

Fundamentals of Fancy Diving.—Just as in swimming, there are definite bases for the development of the fancy forms of diving. Fancy dives are as previously stated variations of position and direction or combinations of both.

From the plain forms of diving the learner must proceed to a series of skills out of which all the fancy dives are developed. The first series consists of the front jackknife, the back dive, the front and back somersaults and the half-twist. The second series involving change of direction is made up of the Isander (half-gainer, flying Dutchman) and the back jackknife.

Front Jackknife Dive.—The front jackknife is a variation in position of a front dive facing the water.

It is done by assuming a jackknife position with the hands touching the front of the lower leg or foot after leaving the take-off point; holding this position an appreciable interval and then snapping out to diving position. It is used in certain forward dives, in some somersaults, in one form of back dive and in one variation of the half-gainer. Its importance in progressive development cannot be overlooked. The learning process is started best from the low springboard and as a variation of the running front header. The key to its mastery lies in using the spring of the board to lift the hips higher than the head. Instead of taking the usual soaring flight with arched back of the running front header, the body is deliberately jackknifed in mid-flight and the hands carried low to meet and touch the lower legs or feet. Both arms and legs are held straight throughout the dive. At first, the learner will do little more than slap the front of the thighs or knees before straightening out for the entry, but gradually the hands will touch lower and lower on the legs and the position will be held for longer intervals. In the first few attempts the learner may find to his distress that he is overthrowing his entry. This is due to the fact that he is dropping his arms and ducking the head to take the jackknife position, instead of bringing the feet up to meet the hands, and facing forward with the head well up. This can be counteracted by taking a few jackknife dives entering the water feet foremost which will, perforce, keep the head where it belongs. It is finally mastered when the diver can lift from the board, take a full jackknife position, hold it through the top of the flight and whip out of it in time to make a clean entry into the water in good head foremost diving position.   (See Fig. 53).

The Back Dive.   This is the first blind dive for the

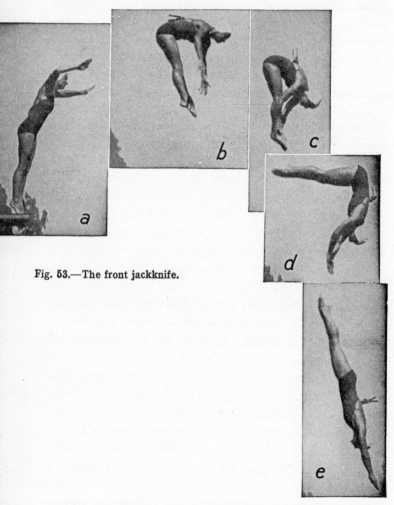

Fig. 53.—The front jackknife.

novice to master. It is termed "blind" because the point of entry cannot be seen until just before the diver touches the water. The first back dive, is perhaps, more difficult for the novice to attempt than any of the others in the series, yet in its simplest form, it is absurdly easy of accomplishment. It is the key to all fancy dives in which the diver enters the water backward. The position is used in the half-gainer, in half and full twists, in the one-and-a-half back and others.

The first attempt requires only that the diver take his position at the end of a spring-board, stretch the arms above the head, arch the back and fall backward. If the head is tilted backward throughout the dive and the feet are left on the board until they are pulled after the falling body, the diver cannot land flat. This is only the initial stage of learning the back dive, however, and after a few attempts have convinced the learner that he will not be hurt, he begins to work on a true back dive.

In the fully co-ordinated back dive, the diver stands at the end of the board well-poised on the balls of the feet. The heels tightly pressed together extend backward over the water. The legs are straight, the body erect and the head in line with the spine. The arms are extended forward at shoulder height and aid in maintaining the balance.

With the down swing of the arms, the diver settles his weight on the end of the board to bend it downward beneath him as deeply as possible. Settling the weight involves sinking the shoulders and lowering the heels as well as swinging the arms downward. As the arms swing forward and upward the diver extends the feet sharply and lifts with the board and then away from it as it reaches the upper limit of its spring. Care must be taken that the diver's center of gravity is slightly beyond the end of the board as he lifts upward to insure clearance of the feet and legs. If the diver's body is swung backward one inch from the

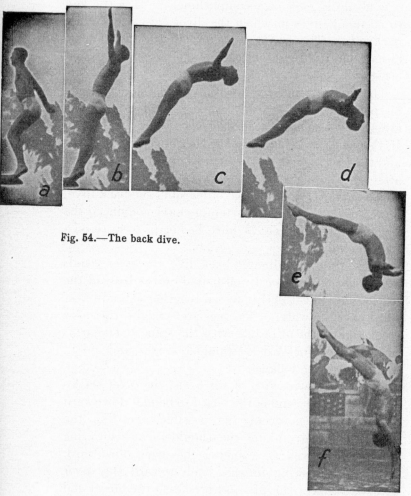

Fig. 54.—The back dive.

perpendicular, his dive will clear the board by three feet no matter how high he may soar.

The flight of a good back dive from a spring-board is not a long arc to the water. It more nearly resembles the flight of a skyrocket in that it soars almost directly upward from the board, turns sharply at the top of the flight and drops back almost per-pendicularly to the water. As the diver leaves the board the arms swing forward, upward over the head which is held in line with the spine. At the top of the dive, the head drops back and the back is arched. The arms may hold the position beyond the head or swing sideward to a swan position in the drop back to the water. If the inverted swan position is taken the arms must be extended beyond the head again before entering the water. The entry should be made at or very close to the perpendicular. (See Fig. 54).

Learning Process for the Backward Dive.—Practice for the back dive beyond the beginner's back fall should start with bounding. Facing the board, the learning diver bounds on the end of the board exactly as he did in learning the running front dive. Balance, poise and timing are developed by this means.

In the first few dives the diver should concentrate on mastery of the co-ordinated lift with little emphasis placed upon getting height. The dive must be brought under control and directed correctly through its flight. It is a common experience in beginning the practice of the back dive to find that most of the first attempts overthrow. This is due to the fact that the diver falls backward from the board and takes its lift on the feet and lower legs rather than the whole body. When balance and poise on the board and in flight are achieved with some measure of control, increasing power can be applied to the spring and lift. It will, however, take considerable practice

before maximum height and precision of entry can
be achieved regularly.

The Forward Somersault.—It is hardly necessary
to define a somersault since almost everyone knows
that it is simply a matter of turning "heels over
head" from one standing position to another.

Front somersaults are done in any one of three
positions; tucked, piked or straight. The tucked
position is one in which the knees are brought to the
chin as the back is rounded and the head tucked well
in. The diver thus revolves swiftly in a compact
bundle. To aid in holding the position the hands
clasp the front of the shins. The pike front somersault
is a revolution in the pike or jackknife position with
one variation; the hands clasp the back of the thighs
just above the knees. It is a somewhat slower turning
movement than the tucked somersault and depends
upon the hunched shoulders and the sharply-dipped
head to take it around. The straight front somersault
in which the body is held rigidly erect throughout
the turn is very difficult to perform and more difficult
to control because of the vigor with which the revolution has to be made.

From low elevations and poorly mounted springboards the tuck form is most generally used. From
well-mounted springboards at standard heights and
from high platforms the somersault in pike position
is more frequently used although for multiple somersaults the tuck position may be employed to better
effect. The open somersault is used only from high
springboards.

The front somersault is an integral part of a good
many fancy dives. It appears in the single, the one-
and-one-half, the two and the two-and-one-half for-

ward somersault dives. It is used in the cutaway one-and-one-half somersault dive and in combination with twists to make still other fancy dives.

Fig. 55.—The front somersault, tucked.

The learning process for the front somersault is most easily begun on land. On sand, soft turf or a gymnasium mat the turn is taken by placing the hands on mat or ground, tucking the chin and rolling over in a tucked position. This is known commonly in gymnastics as the forward roll. When it can be done smoothly and with a good sense of position, it can be done with a little spring and dive. This is

definitely a ground somersault with some portion of
the body in contact at all times with the surface on
which the turn is made.

A very low take-off point should be selected for
the first somersaulting efforts over the water. The
learner leans outward, the shoulders are hunched,
the head tucked in and the shins grasped and the
turnover is made on the way to the water. No
attempt should be made in these initial trials to "open
up" before entering the water and the learner will
make his entry in a compact knot. Only after several
trials will the general bewilderment attendant on the
turning of a forward somersault begin to diminish.
When the learner reaches the point at which he seems
to know where he is at all times during the turn, he
may begin to think about opening up for a clean
entry into the water.

The first attempts to somersault from the springboard either standing or running are quite likely to
overthrow; that is, the learner will spin so rapidly
with the impetus of the lifting board that he will
turn more than a single somersault. If the head is
not tucked well in, the face will receive the full impact
of the contact with the water with very painful and
uncomfortable result. This in itself should indicate
that the learning process must not be hurried; that
time must be taken to get the "feel" of the dive
before the refinements of maximum height, position
and good entry are even considered.

Good form in a front somersault dive consists of
lifting smartly more upward than outward from board
or platform, tucking or piking smoothly and swiftly,
turning completely over and straightening the body
smartly to make a clean entry into the water. The

body should be erect, legs straight and close together with the toes pointed and the fully extended arms should be pressed close to the sides before entering the water. The entry for best form should be at right angles to the surface or just back of it.

The learner should master the "tuck" form before attempting to take the somersault in the pike position. He should turn the somersault at the top of his flight bringing the knees up to meet the chin rather than lunging downward, with the upper body and arms to clutch the shins. The first stages of practice should be confined to low platforms and low springboards. After the somersault is mastered thoroughly, practice can be taken from the high board and the high platform. The single forward somersault from a height is very difficult to control and its performance belongs in the upper brackets of diving skill. The open forward somersault and the flying forward somersault should not be attempted by anyone but the highly skilled diver. (See Fig. 55).

The Backward Somersault.—The backward somersault is, of course, a blind dive as the diver must launch himself from board or platform without being able to see the water. It is harder to attempt but easier to control and, therefore, easier to learn.

This somersault can also be done in three positions; tucked, piked and straight. In the tucked position the knees are under the chin and the shins clasped tightly but the head is thrown back quite unlike the head position in the front somersault. In the piked position the hands clasp the backs of the knees or calves and lift the legs around. The backward layout or straight somersault is much easier of accomplishment than the front somersault in a like position. In it the body is kept fully extended throughout the dive.

The tucked position is used entirely during the learning process and from low elevations and stub springboards. It is employed also for multiple somersaults from the standard low springboard. The pike is used in certain combinations of back somersaults and dives. The layout position is used only after some skill in diving has been developed. It is considered the best form for a single back somersault and is employed in certain combination dives from the high springboard and high platform.

Like the front somersault, the back somersault is a part of many fancy dives. The back one-and-one-half, the half twisting one-and-one-half back, the double back, the Mollberg (full gainer), the one- and one-half and the double gainers should not be attempted unless the back somersault has been mastered.

The learning method for the backward somersault begins most easily on land. From a squatting position on mat or ground, the learner simply sits back, pulls the knees to the chin and rolls over backward to another squatting position. In this phase of the routine of learning, the head is tucked forward to avoid bumping the back of the skull. Standing erect the learner should next practice standing leaps in place. With a lift of the arms, the learner leaps straight upward, bringing the knees to the chin and clasping them with the hands momentarily, then letting go as he drops back in place. This is good practice for tight tucking.

The first attempts to turn the backward somersault are made from a low springboard. If the learner has previously mastered the back dive, the chances are he will be successful with the backward somersault on the very first attempt. Standing in back diving position on the board, the learner starts his lift as though it was to be a back dive. As he leaves the board he lifts the knees to the chin, grasps the shins with the hands and turns over. Even in the first few tries, if he can see the water beneath him as the turn is completed, he can begin to straighten out for entry into the water. With further attempts the body will be brought into line gradually and the entry will be straighter and straighter until the diver is cleaving the surface with body and legs fully extended and vertical and the arms close to the sides. The dive may then be tried in pike position and later "laid out." (See Fig. 56).

The backward somersault in the straight position deserves special attention because it is quite unlike any other form of somersaulting. It requires tremendous "chest expression" to bring the body completely around in fully extended position. As the diver leaves the board, the arms are swung forward, circled outward and flung wide from the shoulders bringing the chest forward and arching the back. The head describes a short arc up and away from the board and the extended body of the diver pivots in a complete circle around the head. In essence it is a back dive done so vigorously that it carries all the way around to enter the water feet instead of head foremost.

The Front Dive with a Half Twist.—The half twist as this dive is most commonly termed is the first of the twist dives to master. All dives in which the diver turns on the long axis of the body are twists or screws and the terms used indicate what action takes place.

Only one method is used in doing this dive. The diver lifts from the take-off point in a forward dive. As he springs clear of board or platform the head is rotated smartly on the neck either to right or left. Without changing the angle or direction of the dive the body turns in mid-air, following the head, until the back is toward the water. The diver then drops downward in back diving position. If the rotation of the head is not enough to pivot the body to the back diving position, one arm can be whipped across the body and upward to meet the other in good entry position. The arm will almost have to be used later on to do the full twist dives. (See Fig. 57).

The twist dives (forward and backward) are used by themselves and in combination with somersaults to make many fancy dives.

There is no good way to start the learning process on land. The dive is tried first from a very low elevation. There will be a tendency at first to jack-knife at the hips as the twist is made which will, of course, make it impossible to do the dive successfully. This should be resisted and the learner must learn to keep the body straight regardless of his qualms about striking flat on the water.

When the learner has some idea of what he is doing and where he is at all times in the dive, it can be taken to the springboard and first, from a standing position and later with a run, it can be practiced and perfected.

Basic Fancy Dives Involving Change of Direction.— The second category of basic dives has only two dives listed in it; the back jackknife and the Isander or half-gainer. These are classified in competitive diving as a front dive facing the board and a back dive facing the water, respectively. The back jackknife is basic to the cutaway somersault dive and the cutaway one-and-one-half somersaults. Out of the Isander is developed the Mollberg somersault (full-

Fig. 56.—The back somersault, tucked.

gainer), the Mollberg one-and-one-half and the Mollberg double somersaults. Some of these dives are characterized as dangerous and have from time to time been ruled out of competition as being perilous to the diver yet they have invariably been brought back again as examples of the finest co-ordinated diving effort of a singular degree of difficulty. A little reflection will show clearly why these dives are considered dangerous. Both categories involve not only accomplishment of the dives but changes in direction.

Thus, a front dive facing the board and a back dive facing the water are directed toward the board and if not lifted outward away from it can well cause the

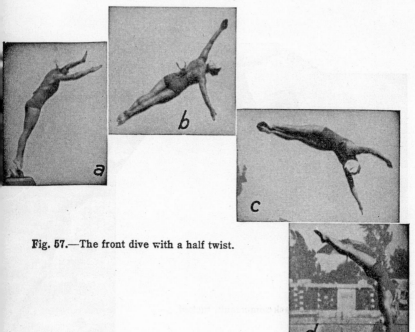

Fig. 57.—The front dive with a half twist.

diver to land not in the water but on or back of his take-off point. The back jackknife is not difficult to learn and is well within the reach of anyone who has some diving sense. The half gainer, however, involves many factors in its successful accomplishment and is not attempted until the learner is well on the way toward becoming a pretty good fancy diver.

Back Jackknife Dive.—In this dive the diver stands well poised on the end of the board exactly as he would for a back header. Leaning slightly backward until

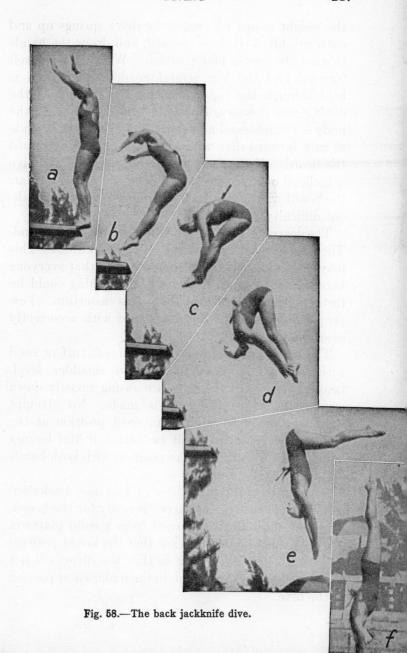

Fig. 58.—The back jackknife dive.

the weight is just off center the diver springs up and
outward, hikes the hips upward, and drops the hands
to meet the toes in pike position. With the head well
forward and the legs straightened, this position is
held through the top portion of the flight. As the
diver drops downward past the end of the board the
body is straightened and entry into the water is made
as in a forward dive with the back, however, toward
the board. If the body at the beginning of the dive
is inclined one inch backward from the perpendicular,
the board will be cleared by as much as two feet without difficulty.

The learning process for this dive begins on land.
The learner must first learn to jump backward. This
may seem too simple, on the assumption that everyone
knows how to jump backward but nothing could be
further from the truth than this assertion. Few
people know how to leap backward with a correctly
co-ordinated spring.

The learner stands well poised on soft turf or sand
with the arms raised forward to shoulder level.
Leaning backward the arms are swung smartly down
and backward as the leap is made. No attempt
should be made to land in an erect position at the
end of the jump. It will be better if the learner
lands bent forward in a pike position with both hands
and feet on the ground.

As soon as a jump of three or four feet backward
can be made easily, the learner is ready for the board.
The dive must not be learned from a solid platform
and care must be taken to see that the board projects
far enough over the water so that the diver will not
strike wall or dock structure in the underwater portion
of the dive.

Position may be taken at one corner of the board and the dive made to one side if the learner feels safer in so doing. If, however, the co-ordination of a backward jump has been well-established there will be no great danger of hitting the board.

The body is well poised at the start just as it is in the back header, the head up, back flat and arms raised forward to shoulder level. To start the dive, the learner sways backward slightly off center, pushes sharply with the feet and swings the arms vigorously downward. The hips are lifted high and the diver heads downward toward the water. From the pike position the legs are whipped back and up and the diver enters the water as in a plain front header back to the board. This will not get great height from the board but it will insure clearance and make a head foremost entry possible. Continued practice dives using this form will develop sureness and a degree of good form in the dive. Later, the arms may swing downward before leaving the board and swing upward with a vigorous shoulder lift to get greater height and, consequently, more time in which to take the pike position and come out of it unhurriedly. Smoothness and grace come with continued practice. (See Fig. 58).

The Isander (**Half-gainer**).—There are a number of ways in which to learn the half-gainer dive. It can be done from a low or high springboard or a high platform. It can be done standing or running, off one foot or both, straight or piked. All require, however, a vigorous lift up and outward from the board to raise the legs and body forward higher than the head and permit the diver to drop back head foremost.

The standing half-gainer from the springboard is selected arbitrarily for description not because it is the simplest but because it has in it all the basic elements, uncomplicated by any other factors.

Standing erect at the end of the board, the diver

Fig. 59.—The half-gainer.

swings the arms downward, settling his weight on the end of the board to bend it downward. As the board lifts beneath him and the arms lift forward-upward, the diver leans slightly forward and projects the front of the hips up and away from the board. The back is arched with the head thrown back and the legs and body swing forward and upward very rapidly. At the top of the dive, the arms are swung to the sides horizontally and the diver assumes a position exactly like that of the swan dive, but upside down. From this position the head and shoulders drop downward past the end of the board and the body and legs follow. The arms are brought forward of the head in the downward flight and entry into the water is made in exactly the same manner as a back header, but facing the board. Good form throughout the dive consists in holding the body in a long smooth curved position, the back arched not too deeply and the legs straight and together. The entry should be clean and at or very close to the vertical. (See Fig. 59).

The learning process begins on land. It is a perfectly natural trait for anyone when he leaps forward to incline the body in the same direction. It is not natural to drop the head and body backward when one is moving forward. To combat this instinct is one of the first requirements of the learning method.

Standing on one foot the learner gets a secure hand hold on something about waist-high. He then practices swinging the other leg forward and dropping the body backward with each forward swing. He should endeavor to see the ground behind him every time the head drops back. When he feels that this co-ordination is well established, the learner is ready to take it to the board. A low springboard is selected for the initial attempts because of the lift it will contribute and because, if the first attempts are not successful, the impact with the surface of the water will not be too great.

Standing at the extreme inboard end of the diving board, the learner *runs* vigorously along the board so spacing his steps that his natural jumping foot lands just back of the outer end of the board at the completion of his last stride. Immediately the other leg swings forward and upward in a vigorous kicking movement as he leaps out into the air. The head is dropped backward and the learner drops backward into the water head foremost regardless of the position of arms or legs. In essence, the learner runs off the end of the board and kicks so hard that he turns himself upside down. It is surprising how many novices are successful in the first try.

While the one foot take-off is not used in formal competition except from high platforms, it can be done in smooth and pleasing form in this manner. The swing forward of one leg, the smooth lift of the other leg to a position parallel with the first and the long slow backward flight to the water when done by an expert is a most pleasing example of fine control. However, since the novice will confine his early efforts to springboards at lower elevations he should learn the prescribed form of take-off for those heights.

After the one foot take-off can be made with ease and assurance, the learner is ready for the next step which is to do the running half-gainer, taking off from both feet. The approach is identical with that for any running front dive and if it is done vigorously, the learner will never strike the board in the dive since the momentum developed in the approach will project him outward and away from it. There must be in the learner's mind a consciousness that he is projecting the front of the hips to the highest point of the dive. If the legs do not follow the flight of the rest of the body readily it may be necessary for the learner to concentrate on lifting the feet rather than the hips. There is a tendency among novices to beat the lift of the board in their eagerness to go into the dive. That is, instead of waiting for the board to spring them into the air, they merely hit it with the feet and go into the dive. This allows for little height and consequently less time in which to pivot into diving position.

Gradually, with continued practice, the novice will become accustomed to this novel dive in which he springs forward but dives backward. Every attempt will bring improvement in height, control and form if it is conscientiously studied. When it is under control and no sooner, it may be attempted from the standing position.

Much space has been given to the discussion of this basic fancy dive because a complete understanding of a safe learning process is necessary to avoid injury. If at times the description may have seemed complicated it should be remembered that the dive itself is complicated. It can not be dealt with as simply as many another dive.

When the learner is master of all the foregoing basic fancy dives as well as the plain forms he is well on the way to becoming a fancy diver. He has the elements out of which every fancy dive in the catalog is made and his progress in diving skill from this time forward can be made in orderly fashion.

As previously pointed out, it is not always possible for every aspiring diver to master all forms of fancy diving because of the limitations put upon him by his physical structure in attempting certain dives. It is not necessary to master all the basic fancy dives to develop considerable diving ability within certain limits. For example, a learner, who is well adapted in physique to twist dives but who may find somersaults difficult to master may develop all the twisting dives and let the somersaults alone. For all-round diving performance, however, all the categories of dives should be exploited.

Fancy diving is above everything else, always interesting and challenging to the learner at any stage of his development. It can begin as soon as he has mastered his first plain header and it has no end. Few indeed are those of whom it can be said "He has mastered and perfected every known form of fancy dive." The learning process can be continued over a period of many years.

Before listing and describing the forms of fancy diving in their respective categories, something must be said about the more difficult dives. It is easy to say, for example, that the diver masters the forward somersault, the forward one-and-one-half, then the double forward somersault and finally the two-and-one-half, but the learning process is not so simple as that. Mentally, the learner must prepare himself for the next form of related fancy dive, even as he is mastering the one with which he is then engaged. Excellent competitive fancy divers have stated that they have, for example, thought over the co-ordination of a two-and-one-half forward somersault dive or a one-and-one-half back, for two years before they ever attempted it. In essence, they have thought all the way through the action and co-ordination of the dive until they have a clear picture of what they propose to do before trying it. The importance of this cannot be discounted if one realizes that once launched from the board, a dive cannot be called back. The learner simply has to go through with it and if he cannot visualize the whole dive, he will, as divers term it, "take a beating," if he doesn't make it.

The fancy dives listed have been placed in five groups. All the forward dives in which the diver faces the water at the beginning of the dive are placed in the first group. All the backward dives in which the diver faces the board are in the second group. The third group is made up of all backward dives in which the diver faces the water. The fourth group includes all forward dives in which the diver faces the board, and the fifth and last set of dives is made up of all the dives in which some form of twist is employed. Every group of dives is arranged progressively from the simplest to the most complex forms. Many dives are listed which are not recognized as standard fancy dives in formal diving competition, but as variations of plain diving, they have their uses. It should not be necessary for a novice to forego the pleasure of informal or formal diving competition until he has mastered certain arbitrarily selected dives. It should be possible for him to vie with his swimming mates in dives coming within the range of his abilities. It may also be noted that many of the simpler fancy dives listed are but steps in the learning process for the more complex forms. All have their place in the development of diving skill and all have their uses.

Fancy Dives

Forward Dives, Diving Facing the Water

Swan Dive.—A head foremost entry dive, standing or running which is simply a variation of the plain front header, in which the arms are held at right angles to the body throughout the flight of the dive. The arms are brought forward of the head just before entering the water. (See Fig. 60).

Swallow Dive.—A header forward standing or running in which the hands rest on the hips until just before entering the water.

Butterfly Dive.—A header forward, standing or running, in which the arms are extended forward and outward at an angle of 45° and the legs are separated and extended backward at a like angle during the dive. Just before entering the water, legs and arms are closed and extended for the usual entry of a plain header.

Soldier Dive.—A header forward, standing, from any reasonable height greater than the length of the diver. From a standing position the arms are fully extended above the head, the diver inclines forward and without springing or bending the body, tilts forward and downward and plunges head foremost from platform or board. Due to the rigidity of the body in this dive, it is sometimes termed the "wooden soldier" or statue dive.

Sailor Dive.—The origin of the name of this dive is unknown but it implies a naval source. It is nothing more than a plain front header taken from a low platform or springboard in which the arms are held fully extended close to the sides through the dive and the entry into the water. Because there is no protection for the head, the impact must be taken on the forehead. In the torpedo position taken the diver often penetrates quite deeply so it is advisable to have at least 12 feet of water beneath the take-off point.

Plunge Dive.—This dive is a plain front header, standing or running, made shallowly at a rather flat

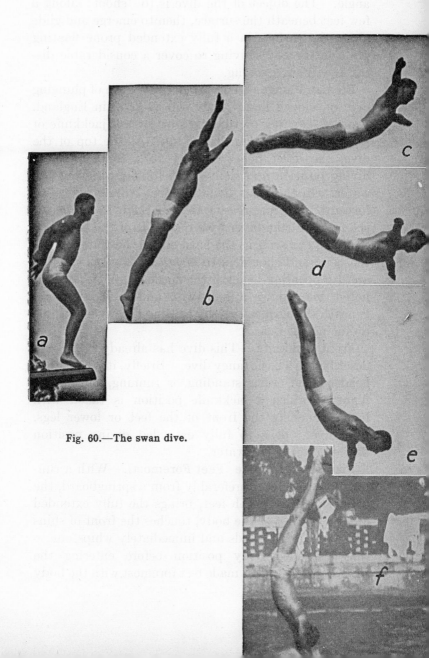

Fig. 60.—The swan dive.

angle. The object of the dive is to "shoot" along a few feet beneath the surface, then to emerge and glide along the surface in a fully extended prone floating position thereby striving to cover a considerable distance without stroking.

Etonian Plunge.—This is a peculiar form of plunging dive developed many years ago at Eton in England. From a standing or running start, a half jackknife or pike position is taken in the air. At the top of the dive, the diver opens smartly to a fully extended diving position and slants head foremost toward the water. In this, it is little different from a pike dive forward. The peculiarity that marks it as distinct is the fact that the diver by a quick lift of the head and stroke of the arms as the head enters the water causes the head and shoulders to emerge almost as the feet are disappearing beneath the surface. A variation is noted in making a half-twist and jackknife bend beneath the surface thereby causing the diver to come up facing the board.

Front Jackknife.—This dive has already been fully described as a basic fancy dive. Briefly, it is a forward header done either standing or running, during the flight of which a jackknife position is taken with hands touching the front of the feet or lower legs. The diver opens to fully extended diving position before entering the water.

Pike Forward Dive (**Feet Foremost**).—With a running approach and preferably from a springboard, the diver leaps from both feet, brings the fully extended legs up in front of the body, touches the front of shins or feet with the hands and immediately whips out to fully extended body position before entering the water. The entry is made feet foremost with the body rigidly erect, arms close to the sides. This is an excellent companion dive for the Pike Forward head foremost and should be practiced alternately with it to develop control of position.

Sitting Jump.—While this is a very elemental diving stunt, it is placed in the fancy diving progression because it marks the first use of the tucked position. With a running approach from low springboard or platform the diver springs upward, tucks the knees beneath the chin and clasps the shins tightly with the arms and hands. The body remains upright and the diver hits the surface of the water in a sitting position. This dive should never be attempted over water less than six feet in depth because of the risk of hitting the bottom in a sitting position with consequent injury to the spine.

A variation of the sitting jump which is a bit more difficult to control is to straighten out immediately following the tuck and enter the water in good feet foremost position.

Cannon Ball Dive.—This dive is the immediate forerunner of the forward somersault. Preferably, from a low springboard and with a running approach, the diver springs out and upward into the air, just as he would for a running front header. Upon leaving the board the knees are brought to the chin and clasped securely by the arms while the head remains up and forward. When the diver inclines toward the water, the body is straightened, the legs extended and a good head foremost entry made.

Forward Somersault.—This has already been described as a basic fancy dive. It may be taken standing or running, tucked or piked. It is recommended that the learner take this dive from low

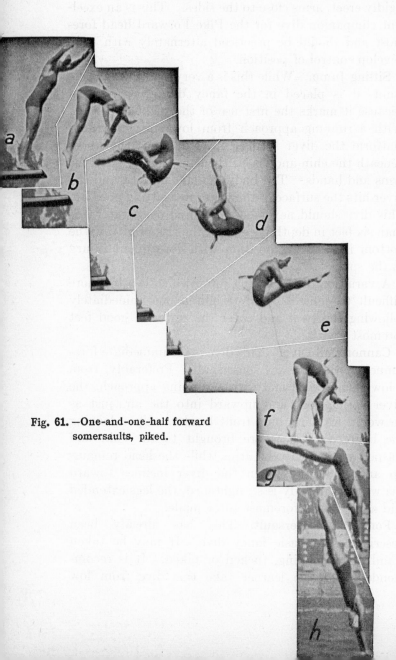

Fig. 61.—One-and-one-half forward
somersaults, piked.

elevations at first and acquire good control before he attempts it from the high springboard and platform. It is very difficult to control from any considerable height above the water.

One-and-one-half Forward Somersault.—The forward somersault and dive is the first of the combined or multiple dives usually attempted by the aspiring fancy diver. It is, as the name implies, a forward somersault turned vigorously to a point at which the diver can straighten out and enter the water head foremost. The tucked form with a running approach on the low springboard is the one usually attempted first. This is one of the many dives in which the diver must think the co-ordination through before trying it. First attempts are usually "scrambled" in appearance and utterly bewildering to the novice diver but with repeated tries awareness of position develops surprisingly soon. Once the feeling of the dive is established, it can be practiced for height and good form and then may be tried standing and running, from platform and springboard, high and low, tucked and piked. From low elevations the spring into the air will be vigorous, the turn rapid. From greater heights the leap will be modified, the turn slower. Continued practice at varying heights will develop a sense of the "timing" necessary for the type of take-off, the height and the form used.

Forward Double Somersault.—The Double Somersault Forward is done simply by continuing the one-and one-half for another half turn. Instead of breaking out to a dive at the completion of the first one the somersaulting position is held until another complete turn has been made to enter the water feet foremost.

In most cases, it is learned most easily in tucked position from a low springboard and always with a running approach. At first, no attempt is made to straighten out at the completion of the second somersault, the entry being made as in a sitting jump. It will be found that if the turns are made with the utmost vigor, the diver will just about complete two revolutions before striking the water. When some sense of position has developed, the diver may straighten the body at the completion of the second somersault to make a clean feet foremost entry. When it is under control, this dive may be taken to the high springboard and the pike form used in the somersaults.

Two-and-one-half Forward Somersault.—The fancy divers who can turn two-and-one-half somersaults from a low springboard consistently can be numbered on the fingers of the hands. Those who can accomplish it from the high springboard and high platform are not numerous. This dive may be said to be the most difficult of all forward dives facing the water. It should, therefore, be tried only after the diver has thoroughly mastered the preceding dives. Its name describes it; simply, two complete somersaults forward finishing with another half-turn and a head foremost dive. It is learned with less difficulty from the high springboard but little can be said about the learning process. The diver may think this dive through for a period of months and a day may come when he feels that he can do it. Only one thing can be said about the first trials and that is to let the first somersault take care of itself and to concentrate on turning the second and the half. The tuck is used while learning and only after full mastery of the dive in that position, is the pike attempted.

Flying Forward Somersault.—One of the most beautiful and difficult of all fancy dives is the Flying

Forward Somersault done from the high platform. From the ten meter elevation it is attempted only by the most highly skilled fancy divers but from the high springboard it can be attempted by those possessed of some fancy diving ability.

It is done with a running approach and the diver leaves the board as though he were doing a running front header. As the top of the flight is reached and the dive turns downward, the diver folds into a compact knot and turns a very rapid forward somersault. When the somersault is completed the diver straightens out and continues in the same line of flight to enter the water feet foremost.

BACKWARD DIVES, DIVER FACING THE BOARD

Backward Header.—Of all the backward dives this is the simplest form. The dive has been fully described heretofore as a basic fancy dive. Little more may be said about it except to state that the correct "timing" is the essence of control and good form in the backward header. On the low springboard a maximum effort will just about put the diver in position for a clean entry into the water. From the high board and platform, however, there is a noticeable delay at the top of the dive, in dropping the head backward to take the arched position lest the diver overthrow and land on the front.

Pike Back Dive.—An interesting variation of the plain backward header and one seldom used is the Pike Back Dive. The diver starts as for a backward dive, springs up and outward, takes a well defined pike position at the top of the dive then whips out to the back diving position again to enter the water head foremost.

Backward Somersault.—The Backward Somersault
has already been discussed as a basic fancy dive. It
can be done in three ways: tucked, piked, or straight
from platform or springboard at almost any height.
The "lay-out" or open position is the most graceful
manner in which it can be done.

Backward One-and-one-half Somersault.—Although the Backward Double Somersault is actually
easier to learn than the Backward One-and-one-half,
the latter is placed ahead of the former in the learning
progression because it is easier to develop it out of
the single backward somersault than it is to come back
to it after mastering the double spin.

The Backward One-and-one-half Somersault is a
truly difficult dive to control because the breakout to
the diving position from the somersault is in line with
and a continuation of the direction of the somersault
itself quite unlike the Forward One-and-one-half in
which the breakout to the dive is opposed to the
direction of the spin. Furthermore, the Backward
One-and-one-half is a blind dive. So in this dive the
learner has little margin one way or another in the
brief interval in which he is to open from the spinning
somersault to the dive. He must break out of the
somersault to the dive much sooner than he wants to
in order to allow for a continuation of the spinning
momentum which he cannot entirely check by opening
to diving position. Thus, it can be said that a diver
attempting the Backward One-and-one-half Somersault must spin smartly either tucked or piked and
when he has almost completed the somersault should,
by throwing the head and arms backward, arching
the spine and extending the legs smartly, check the
momentum of his spin as much as possible and drop

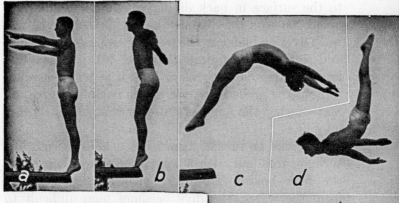

Fig. 62.—One-and-one-half backward
somersaults, straight.

to the surface in back diving position. If the diver opens too soon the dive will be flat; if too late he will wash over and land on the front. As a safety measure and to avoid discomfort, the diver will minimize the impact either on the back or front if he will remember to hold the arched position of the backward dive, no matter what the angle of entry or complete lack of it may be.

The pike or tucked form is used always from low springboards and with a somewhat slower spin from the high board. However, with increasing height from the water, the dive becomes more difficult to control in either of these positions. It is customary, therefore, among the better fancy divers to use the straight position for the Backward One-and-one-half Somersault from the three meter springboard and from the ten meter platform. This is undoubtedly the most beautiful form in which this dive can be done. The diver leaves his take-off and arching vigorously does a whipping, pivoting lay-out somersault with so much momentum that the somersault continues on into a back dive without changing the position of the body. This represents the acme of timing and control especially from the high platform and is not attempted until the learner is in the "top flight" of fancy divers. (See Fig. 62).

Backward Double Somersault.—The Backward Double Somersault is but a continuation of the Backward One-and-one-half in the learning process. The diver starts as for a One-and-one-half but instead of breaking out to a dive after one somersault is completed, continues in the tucked or piked position until he has completed a second somersault. As the second somersault is completed, the body is straight-

ened and the diver enters the water feet foremost.
This dive is seldom done effectively from the low
springboard because of the lack of time in which to
spin twice and straighten out but the double turn can
be learned there with the diver entering the water in a
sitting position. When timing and control are established it can be taken to the high board and perfected.
It is not turned from the high platform because of the
danger involved.

A form of the Backward Double Somersault from
the high board which is rarely seen but which is
extremely graceful is to turn the first somersault very
tightly tucked high above the board and then to
break out and turn the second one laid out. In the
second somersault the diver seems to float downward
through the air.

Flying Backward Somersault.—Like the Flying
Forward Somersault this dive starts with a well
pointed header, but backward. A tightly tucked
backward somersault is turned as the diver turns
downward toward the water which is opened at its
completion to continue feet foremost for entry into
the water.

FRONT DIVES, DIVER FACING BOARD OR PLATFORM

Back Jackknife.—This dive has already been
described as the basic fancy dive for the category in
which the diver projects himself up and backward
but dives toward the take-off point. In learning
this group of dives great care should be taken to spring
backward far enough to clear the edge of the take-off.
All these dives must be done standing so the momentum of a running approach is, perforce, eliminated
as a safety factor.

Cutaway Somersault.—The Cutaway Somersault may be made from the low or high springboard and from the high platform. From the low board the tucked form is generally used; from the other heights the pike position is taken. On the low board where the learning process usually starts, the dive requires for successful completion that the diver leap backward and up as for a back jackknife, bring the knees to the chin and simultaneously whip the arms downward vigorously and duck the head and shoulders down and under the tucked body. This action serves to turn a forward somersault toward the board even while the diver is still above his take-off point. As soon as the somersault is completed, the body and legs are straightened to enter the water feet foremost. From greater heights the ducking action is less vigorous and the somersault is turned in the pike position. (See Fig. 63).

Cutaway One-and-one-half Somersault.—This dive is performed most frequently from the three meter springboard and is best learned from that height because of the fraction of increase in the time it takes for the flight of the dive. From the low board, a cutaway one-and-one-half somersault demands extraordinary agility to accomplish. From the high board and the high platform, this is another dive the difficulty of which automatically puts it in the top flight of dives, to be undertaken only by the most advanced divers.

Briefly, the dive may be described as a cutaway somersault turned either in tucked or piked position so vigorously that the diver makes not only a forward somersault but another half turn to a head downward position from which he opens out to enter the water in good head foremost diving position.

Cutaway Double Somersault.—This is a dive of

Fig. 63.—The cutaway somersault, piked.

extreme difficulty, which is hardly possible of accomplishment on a low board, and is turned from the high board or the high platform only by the most expert fancy divers. All that can be said about it is that it is one step beyond the cutaway one-and-one-half. Two consecutive somersaults are turned rapidly enough

Fig. 64.—Gainer somersault, tucked.

to enable the diver to straighten out before reaching the water and to enter in a good feet foremost position.

Back Dives, Diver Facing the Water

The back dives facing the water are few in number and somewhat difficult to master. The Isander (half-gainer) has been described previously as a basic fancy dive in which the diver springs forward from board or platform and dives backward.

Pike Isander (Pike Half-gainer).—This is an interesting variation of the Isander. In doing it the diver springs up and away from the board and assumes a pike position. The body is jackknifed, and the legs extended and the feet brought up to touch the hands on a level with the eyes. Immediately, the diver whips out of the pike position and drops backward to enter the water as in the Isander. It can be done standing or running.

Mollberg Somersault (Full gainer).—The simplest way to describe the Mollberg is to term it a backward somersault which gains distance forward as it is turned. It can be done standing or running, from board or platform, off one or both feet. The tuck, pike, or lay-out position may be taken in executing this dive. The tucked form is used in learning the dive and generally when doing the Mollberg from a low springboard. From the high board and platform, the piked position is generally taken but the form considered to be the best and the one used by the most expert fancy divers is the lay-out or straight position. The somersault should be completed high enough above the water to allow time enough for the diver to straighten out for good feet foremost entry into the water. (See Fig. 64).

One-and-one-half Mollberg Somersault.—This dive is a complete Mollberg somersault continuing into a backward header. It is considered one of the most difficult of all fancy dives to master and is attempted only by the most expert fancy divers. Like the Backward One-and-one-half Somersault, its difficulty lies in its control. Good judgment of position in the air is necessary to determine when the diver should break out of the somersault and go into backward diving position. It can be done standing or running, off one foot or both, from low and high springboards or high platforms. The tuck or pike form can be used from any or all heights. The straight position can be used from the high springboard or high platform.

Double Mollberg Somersault.—This is two consecutive reverse somersaults turned with vigor either in the tucked or piked position from the high springboard or the high platform. It is less difficult to accomplish and control than the One-and-one-half Mollberg.

TWIST DIVES

Screw or twist dives are aptly named since the turning action on the long axis of the body as it travels through the air is a rotating advancing motion. In simplest form it is the running leap with the half-turn toward the take-off point so often seen performed by children who have just learned to dive. For many it is the first conscious variation of plain diving.

Front Dive, One-half Twist.—This dive has been discussed fully as a basic fancy dive. Its mastery comes first in the category of screw or twisting dives. Done correctly from a high board it is a beautiful and graceful form of diving.

Front Jackknife, Half-twist.—The Front Jack-knife with a half-twist has two forms, one of which is recognized as standard for competitive fancy diving. The other form is a variation useful in gaining control of position. The first form is completed head foremost, the second enters the water feet foremost.

In the front jackknife, half-twist, the diver springs into the air taking the pike position. Then as the diver opens out to diving position, one shoulder is dropped and the head is rotated smartly over the lowered shoulder so that the diver is looking backward. The entry is made head foremost back to the board or platform.

The front Jackknife, One-half Twist, with a feet foremost entry is done by piking the feet and hands forward in front of the eyes and rotating the head smartly right or left to make a half turn as the body and legs are extended. The entry is made feet foremost facing the take-off point.

Front Jackknife Full Twist.—A running approach is usually taken for this dive and the pike position is held but briefly. As soon as the body and legs are fully extended after the pike, the head is rotated vigorously and one arm is swept across in front of the body to aid in the turning movement. A full turn is made and the diver enters the water head foremost fronting the take-off point.

Front Dive, Full Twist.—In this dive, the diver leaves the board and soars upward in swan position. At the top of the dive one arm is bent at the elbow, thrust in and across the chest and then extended parallel to the other arm beyond the head. The head meanwhile rotates smartly in the same direction as the thrusting arm. This action causes the body to make one full revolution, front to back to front and ends in a forward dive. Care must be taken to hold the body and legs vigorously extended throughout the dive. (Fig. 65).

Forward Somersault, One-half Twist.—The diver leaves the board in the same position as for a lay-out forward somersault. After leaving the board, the axis of the shoulders is tilted to lower one and swing the other forward across the line of flight. Thus the diver pivots to face about and to enter the water feet foremost facing his take-off.

Forward One-and-one-half Somersault, One-half Twist.—This is a forward somersault and a half in which a half revolution is made after the somersault is completed, to enter the water as a backward header. The diver will find it a relatively easy step from the One-and-one-half Forward Somersault to this dive. At the point where the diver breaks out of the somersault to diving position, one shoulder is dropped and the head rotated until the diver is looking back over it. This is done either from the tuck or pike position.

Full Twisting Forward, One-and-one-half Somersaults.—The dive indicated is done with a running approach generally from the high springboard or high platform. A forward somersault half-piked or straight in which the diver, by a whip of the arms and shoulders and a full circle of the head, makes a full turn of the body, is the first portion of the dive. To finish it, the somersault is turned so vigorously that when the twist and the somersault are completed, the diver continues to turn until he is head downward and ready to make a good head foremost entry into the water. The dive is a half-piked one-and-one-half forward somersault in which the diver makes one full twist while he is somersaulting.

Backward Header, One-half Twist.—This is a simple variation of the backward header in which the diver starts a back dive and at the top of his flight, by whipping one arm across the chest and rotating the head on the neck, turns about and drops back to the water to enter as in a forward header.

Backward Header, Full Twist.—The full twist in the backward header is a continuation of the foregoing half-twist. The twist starts just after the diver leaves the board and is accomplished almost entirely by a vigorous circling of the head and shoulder. It starts as a backward header, turns forward and continues to a position back to the water and enters as in a backward header.

Backward Somersault, One-half Twist.—This and the following dive are most easily accomplished as developments of the straight backward somersault. When the straight backward somersault is mastered it is relatively easy to impart a lateral spin to the body as the somersault is turned by turning the head and shoulders to one side or the other. The dive finishes feet foremost with the back to the board.

Backward Somersault, Full Twist.—If the preceding dive is given a little greater lateral spin by turning the head and shoulders more smartly, a full twist will be imparted to the somersault which will cause the diver to finish his somersault and enter the water facing his take-off point.

Half Twisting Backward One-and-one-half Somersaults.—If the backward lay-out somersault with a half twist is turned from the high springboard or high platform with a more vigorous somersaulting spin, the diver will not only complete the somersault and face about but will pivot far enough to enter the water head foremost. From the low springboard, it is better accomplished by tucking in the somersault.

Back Jackknife, One-half Twist.—This dive is best described as a back jackknife with a half turn entering the water facing the board. As the diver whips out of the pike position he imparts a spin to the straightened body by circling the head and looking back over one shoulder.

Back Jackknife, Full Twist.—A little more vigor in the turn of the head in the preceding dive and it is possible from the high board at any rate, to make a full revolution of the body and enter the water back to the board. Few fancy divers fully master this dive.

Isander, (Half-gainer) One-half Twist.—This is, when done from the high springboard or platform perhaps the most beautiful of the whole list of fancy dives. With a running approach the diver lifts up and outward in the reverse swan position. At the top of his dive, he seems to hang suspended for a moment, then with a swift turn of the head, the body rotates fully laid out and still in the swan position, faces the take-off and seems to float downward past it to enter the water in good head foremost diving position. (See Fig. 66).

Diving Equipment

Plain diving requires little more than a firm base from which to take off and a sufficient depth of water to check the force of the downward plunge and neutralize it. Under low platforms, floats and low springboards eight feet of water should be considered the minimum for all-round safety. As the novice develops skill in the plain dives, however, he may with impunity dive from a solid base into as little as

Fig. 65.—Front dive, full twist.

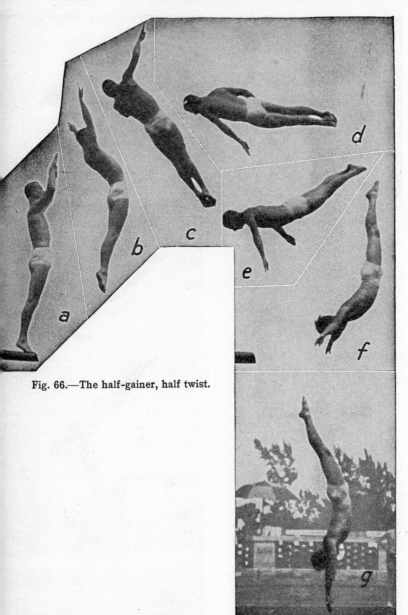

Fig. 66.—The half-gainer, half twist.

five feet of water provided he can do the long shallow
plunging type of dive which penetrates only a little
way beneath the surface. At a height of ten feet
for plain diving there should be at least ten feet of
water into which to plunge. For heights above that
point, the water should increase correspondingly
until a maximum depth of 16 feet is attained. This
depth is ample to insure that the diver will not dash
himself against the bottom no matter what height he
may elect to dive from.

The rules governing fancy diving competition have
rather arbitrarily fixed certain heights for springboards
and platforms and definite minimum depths beneath
them. Although the standards were set to govern
competition, it happens that they are rather good
ones which can well apply to any equipment recommended for fancy diving.

Thus, it has been determined that fancy diving
should be limited to springboards fixed at two levels;
the low board placed one meter (39.37 inches) above
the surface and the high board at three meters (9.83
plus feet). Beneath the low board a minimum depth
of eight feet is required while the minimum depth for
the high board is ten feet. Likewise platforms are
standardized for fancy diving from rigid bases, at five,
eight and ten meters with a minimum depth of 15 feet
indicated. These are good standards since the low
board permits the diver to learn and perform most of
the listed fancy dives at a safe height. The high board
makes it possible for the diver to do all the listed fancy
dives and to have more time in his flight from the board
to the water, in which to accomplish them. It is logical
for the diver as his skill increases to move up to the high
board from the low one. The impact on the surface of

the water will be a little greater at this height but his knowledge of timing and of saving himself bad blows through ill-judged attempts quite offsets the difference in shock. Certainly no diver should use the high board until he is thoroughly familiar with fancy diving at the one meter height.

The graduated levels of the platforms, likewise represent an ascending scale of diving skill as well as heights. No one should attempt to dive from the platforms until he is thoroughly versed in diving from the boards. Furthermore, the upper levels should be reserved to those who have proven diving skill.

If anything is to be added to this scale of heights for diving, it is to place a springboard at the height of 18 to 24 inches for novice springboard diving and possibly to place an intermediate board at the six foot level. No springboard should be placed at a higher level than three meters since if a dive goes out of control the impact with the surface of the water may be too violent for safety. Platforms at greater heights than ten meters are the exclusive right of trained and greatly skilled high divers.

Springboards.—Springboards are resilient pieces of wood so constructed and mounted that they impart a lift to dives done from them which enables the diver to project himself a little higher into the air and thereby have a little more time in which to perform the dive.

The best and most serviceable type of diving board is the one recommended as standard for competitive diving. This board is made of one clear piece of Oregon pine or fir. It has a minimum length of 14 and a maximum of 16 feet and is 20 inches wide. It tapers from a thickness of three inches at the butt end to one-and-one half inches at the diving end. This tapering thickness gives a resilience to the board that a board of uniform thickness throughout its length does not possess. Not only is it strong but its lift is whip-like in character insuring a maximum of height in the dive. Such a board is tapered on the underside only, leaving the top level. Boards of this kind can be made out of other woods, notably oak or second-growth ash but it is difficult to find timber of this kind large enough from which to get a clear piece twenty inches wide. Serviceable boards can be made, however, from timber as short as 12 feet and as narrow as 15 inches but anything shorter or narrower than these is not recommended except as stub boards for novice diving.

Another type of board which is used with considerable success in many places is the composite board made up of three, four, or five longitudinal strips cleated together on the under side. Where wide pieces of timber are difficult to secure, this is one way of using several narrow pieces to get the desired width. In the best of the manufactured boards of this type, the strips are tapered on the under side from butt to tip in the same manner as the standard boards. The one major difficulty presented in boards of this kind is that the outside strips tend to weaken and droop at the outer end which imparts a torque to the diving board and tends to throw the diver sidewise in his dives.

Still another type of diving board is seen occasionally which has little or no spring in itself. This rigid piece of timber relies for its lift on a coiled spring arrangement at the fulcrum of its mounting. Boards of this type are not satisfactory; first, because those

manufactured thus far are too narrow as a rule,
second, because they are badly mounted at too great
a pitch, and third, because they spring but do not
whip the diver upward to secure maximum height.
Until these structural difficulties are overcome they
are not recommended for use.

Diving Board Mounting.—Springboards for best
results should be mounted on rigid structures. Docks
and platforms set on horses, legs or piers are best
suited to this purpose. It is recommended that diving
boards should not be mounted on floating structures
unless the float is so large and so heavy that it offers
a non-swinging, little yielding base. It is estimated
that from thirty to seventy-five percent of the spring
of a board is neutralized by the instability of small
floats. Good or even safe diving is impossible under
such conditions.

Springboards are secured by bolts or lag screws
at the butt end, rest at some point along their length
on a fulcrum and project beyond the extreme outer
side of the structure on which they are mounted, a
distance of at least one meter.

The butt of the board is best secured by placing
across it an iron strap two or three inches in width
and one-quarter to three-eighths of an inch thick.
This strap should extend far enough on either side of
the board to permit bolts to be put through the ends
and secured to the dock or platform structure. Bolts
or lag screws should never be put through the butt of
a good springboard.

The fulcrum is placed somewhere about midway
of the board. If the fulcrum is placed too far forward
of the middle point it tends to make the board stiff
and its action becomes more of a quick snap. If it

is located too far back of mid-board, its reaction to the diver's weight will be slow. The best way in which to determine the point at which the fulcrum is to be located is to secure the butt, place the fulcrum at about the point where judgment says it should be and then have a diver of average weight bound on the end of the board. The fulcrum may be shifted to the point at which the diver seems to get the best results and may then be secured to the deck.

The top of both fulcrum and base should be practically level so that the board will project almost straight out above the water. For safety in fancy diving a springboard should not rise more than two inches in its entire length. It is customary in mounting homemade springboards to pitch the board at too great an angle. If the deck on which the board is mounted is but a few inches above the surface it is the usual practice to secure the base and then build up the fulcrum so as to have the tip of the board at the desired height above the surface. This is a bad and dangerous practice as approaching on a high pitched board is difficult and the spring of the board tends to throw the diver toward his take-off point rather than away from it. Obviously, the thing to do to get the desired height is to build up both the fulcrum and base equally and cross brace between them if necessary.

Indoor mountings should have a clearance between the ceiling and the top surface of the board of not less than twelve feet above the highest board. Girders and truss frames if lower than the ceiling should be located not nearer than ten feet out from the tip end of the board and five feet inward from the take-off point.

All diving boards except composite or built-up boards manufactured with board, fulcrum and base as a single unit, should rest free on the fulcrum. Bolting or strapping the board to the fulcrum does two things. First, it automatically limits the springing quality to the portion of the board projecting beyond the fulcrum and second, it creates a point of maximum stress over the fulcrum which results in very rapid crystallization and weakening of the wood fiber at that point resulting in early breakage.

Diving Platforms.—Diving platforms or towers may be erected at any point where there is sufficient clearance overhead and water of sufficient depth, except over diving boards. There is too much danger of collision between divers and those swimming back to the dock to permit such a concentration of diving equipment.

For ordinary plain forms of diving a platform three to four feet square, railed about on three sides is sufficient, but for platform fancy diving in which a large number of the dives are done with a running approach, a suitable runway must be provided. The platform structure should be provided with a stout ladder and its forward edge should either overhang the dock or deck or be placed so close to it that if a diver falls accidentally he will land in the water.

Platforms at heights greater than ten feet are not recommended for general use but for high fancy diving the structure recognized as standard for competitive fancy diving is recommended. Here three platforms are arranged preferably in a lateral offset at heights of five, eight and ten meters. Each one is a platform, at least two meters wide and five meters long. The ten meter platform must project at least three meters beyond the edge of the pool or deck. The eight meter platform must project two meters and the lowest platform at least one meter beyond the margin of the water.

Covering for Springboards and Platforms.—Springboards and platforms used for diving become slippery when wet and furnish such insecure footing that falls and injuries may result unless they are covered with some material which affords good traction for wet feet. Cocoa-matting is probably the best material to use for this purpose. It is a coarse woven material the surface of which does not become slippery or slimy. Because of its open texture it dries out rapidly and, more important, allows the board beneath it to dry thoroughly when not in use. Springboards and platforms should be covered over their whole length but not necessarily in their entire width. It is customary to stretch strips 18 to 20 inches in width centered along the board or platform and to secure them firmly at their ends. Heavy canvas duck may be used if cocoa-matting is not available. It will be less satisfactory than the matting but quite safe. Corrugated rubber matting while giving good traction and secure footing is not recommended because water which seeps under it does not readily dry out and thereby causes rapid rotting and deterioration of the board itself.

Care and Maintenance of Diving Equipment.—Good diving equipment is costly. Materials which go into the erection of diving board and platform mountings should be stout and the structures well made. "Knocked together" structures deteriorate rapidly and the expense of renewal is far greater than that of good initial construction. Furthermore, the danger of injury due to impaired structure is great in poorly built and constructed equipment. Screws and bolts should be used in preference to nails and spikes, and paint of good quality or creosote should be used to preserve the wood.

First-class springboards of standard type should not be overworked or abused. If properly mounted and cared for they will last for many years. For every springboard in use throughout the year, there should be a board in reserve because springboards in constant use get "tired"; that is, the fibers lose some of their elasticity, probably due to the penetration of moisture into the wood. So, boards should be alternated every three months. The board withdrawn from service should be laid away in a dry place to dry out, rest and recover some of its resiliency. Springboards at outdoor swimming places should be dismounted at the end of the season and stored for the winter months. Several coats of hot linseed oil may be given unpainted boards, just before they are put back into service, to aid in their preservation.

Box Springboards.—Box boards are seen occasionally in summer camps but are by no means common in their distribution. A box board is a springboard over which a small platform is rigged. This platform is placed from three to four feet back of the tip of the springboard and is about three feet in height. Instead of making a running approach to get height in which to do plain or fancy dives, the diver leaps from the platform onto the end of board and dives. The board must be strong to withstand the force of the jump. In this manner, tremendous height in the dives can be attained. The box board should not be used by fancy divers constantly as it

tends to lessen the diver's natural spring but it is good
fun to play on occasionally.

Trapeze and Flying Rings.—The trapeze and the
flying rings require a suspension point well out over
the water and a starting platform which juts beyond
the margin of pool or dock. In pools, they can be
attached to girders or trusses. Over open water a
high and wide frame work must be provided. The
suspension ropes should be of such length that when
the trapeze or rings are swung toward the platform the
arc of the swing will bring them within the diver's
reach at a point just above and a little in front of the
head as he stands on the starting platform. Linked
steel eyes should be used at the points of suspension;
the ropes should never be tied in a loop around the
suspending member, as the friction developed will
quickly wear through the fibers.

General Information on Diving Equipment.—Diving
either of the plain or fancy variety is deservedly popular among swimmers, especially the younger group.
Wherever it is possible more than the customary one
or two springboards should be provided at swimming
places. In small indoor swimming pools, it is hardly
practical to provide for more than one or at most two
springboards but in the larger pools and at out-of-
door bathing places ample diving facilities can be
provided. Boards and platforms should be so arranged
that no two of them have the same point of entry
into the water for the divers. (One should never be
placed directly above another, for instance.) Ten
feet between usual entry points is not too great a
margin for safety. Ladders by which the diving deck
may be regained should be placed several feet to one

side or the other of the take-off points so that the diver will not find it necessary to swim back directly beneath the board or platform.

One rule of safety governs the avoidance of collision and injury among divers using a single board or platform in turn. NEVER START A DIVE UNTIL THE PRECEDING DIVER HAS COME TO THE SURFACE AND MOVED OUT OF RANGE.

Variations of Position and Acrobatics on Springboard

Heretofore only the usual positions facing or back to the water and the free running approach have been discussed in relation to maneuvers on the board. Now, a whole category of things done on the board preliminary to the dive must be discussed. With the exception of one variation in position, the hand stand, no form of acrobatics on the board is recognized in formal diving competition, nevertheless such forms have been developed and are in constant use either for amusement, for novice grades of competition or for exhibition. Many of them are simple and offer good practice in the development of balance, co-ordination and control, while others are difficult of accomplishment. Many of these forms are listed herewith.

Sideward Dive.—This is the simplest variation of position on the board. The diver stands sideward on the take-off and does a sideward dive, bending the body laterally in the flight through the air. If this dive is twisted a little backward in flight it can well be a quarter step toward mastery of the half and full twists.

Mercury Dive.—The Mercury Dive, so-called, is an elementary balancing stunt. The diver stands facing the water and raises one fully extended leg forward to hip level. Maintaining the balance on one foot, the lifted leg is circled out and backward as the body is inclined forward. At the conclusion of this movement, the diver will be standing on one foot with the body and other leg fully extended and angled toward the water. The diver then tips forward and as he leaves the board brings the legs together and enters head foremost in good diving position with the arms extended beyond the head.

Turtle Dive.—The diver crouches on a low elevation facing the water with the knees under the chin, the arms clasping the lower legs and the head tucked well in. In a compact knot the diver over-balances forward and plops into the water much as a turtle slips off a log.

Seal Dive.—On a smooth surface, the diver stretches at full length with the arms fully extended beyond the head, the hands grasping the edge of the dock, swimming pool deck or board. In the prone position, the diver slides forward on the belly by pulling with the hands and as the upper body passes beyond the edge, the diver tilts downward and glides into the water in much the same manner as a seal slips from its rock into the surf.

Jackknife Seal Dive.—From the same starting position as in the preceding dive, the diver pulls himself forward but as he slides he lifts the hips and comes to a jackknife position with only the hands and the front of the feet touching the board. As a continuation of this movement the diver over-balances forward and slips head foremost into the water extending the body and legs as he drops downward.

Rocker Dive.—The Rocker Dive is one of the very first variations of the plain header from a diving board and is very popular among children. The diver takes a sitting position facing the water on the extreme forward end of the springboard. The hands grasp the corners of the board and the diver rocks backward to a position on the back bringing the legs up over the head until the toes touch the board beyond the head. The diver then rocks forward, over-balances and enters the water head foremost.

Head Stand, Back Fall.—If a person can stand on the head on land, he can make a fancy dive of his feat. Placing a towel for a pad at the extreme tip of the springboard the diver places the head upon it and grasps the edges of the board with the hands about two feet back from the head. He then presses or thrusts the legs upward and assumes a head stand position. Over-balancing forward, the diver arches the back, lets go the hand hold and overturns to enter the water feet foremost.

Handspring.—The Handspring from the springboard should be preceded by some practice on land. When the turn can be made somewhat effectively it may be taken to the board. With a walking or running approach of one or two steps, the diver rocks the body forward and places the hands on or grasps the extreme forward edge of the board. As a continuation of this movement the legs are whipped up over the head, the back arched and the arms held rigid. The diver carries over and enters the water in good feet foremost position.

Hand Stand Dive.—All dives from the hand stand position require that the diver has strength enough in the arms to support the entire weight and a sense of balance in this inverted position. The hand stand should be learned on land before it is ever tried on the diving board or platform. On soft sand, on turf, or a gymnasium mat it can be developed most easily against a wall. The hands are placed about 18 inches from the wall and, keeping the head well forward over the hands, the learner presses or thrusts with the feet and allows the legs to swing up and over until the feet touch the vertical surface. The center of gravity and the position may then be so adjusted that the body is balanced over the hands without touching the wall with the feet.

In the hand stand dive, the diver grasps the corners or the leading edge of the board or platform and swings up to a hand stand position. This point of balance is held for an appreciable interval and then the body is allowed to lean outward. As the balance is lost, the hands press away and are brought forward beyond the head as the diver shoots perpendicularly downward head foremost.

Hand Stand, Back Fall.—This is a variation of the preceding dive in which the diver over-balances from the hand stand position and, instead of thrusting away from the board as in the hand stand dive, falls backward to enter the water feet foremost.

Standing-sitting Dive (Spanker).—As a thing of no great beauty this dive has found little favor among swimming authorities and teachers, yet it persists as a variation of plain diving and a stunt of considerable interest to novice divers. It requires a rather flexible springboard especially for children by whom it is most frequently done.

Standing at the tip of the board, facing the water, the diver slips his feet forward and lands in a sitting position on the spot where he has just been standing. If the muscles are tensed, the board will be pressed downward by his weight and will lift sharply again.

As the board rises beneath him, the diver leans outward and tips into a head foremost dive.

Standing-sitting-standing Dive.—This is the same as the Standing-sitting dive in its first part, but instead of tipping off the board from the sitting position, the diver returns to a standing position before taking the dive.

A variation of this dive is performed by making a half-turn of the body in rising to the standing position again, thereby turning the back to the water and finishing with either a backward somersault or backward dive.

Standing-sitting, Back Somersault.—In this dive, the diver sits at the tip of the board facing inward and measures off the length of his extended legs on the board. He then takes a standing position at the point to which his feet extended. Still facing inboard, he sits back with legs straight, jackknifing the body slightly forward at the same time. When the hips contact the board the head and upper body are thrown back and the diver continues into a backward somersault entering the water feet foremost.

Forward Roll Dive.—At a point far enough back of the tip of the board to insure that the turn will bring the diver to the end of the board at its completion, the diver crouches and rolls over in a forward somersault. As the turn is completed he continues off the end of the board, in a forward dive from the sitting position.

Hand Stand, Forward Somersault.—This is a somewhat difficult dive done usually from the high platforms. The hand stand position is taken and carried over into a pike position for a full forward somersault ending in a forward dive. This is not a one-and-one-half somersault as commonly supposed, but a single somersault starting from a hand stand position and finishing as a forward dive.

Hand Stand and Forward Cut Through.—This is one of the more difficult dives done from the high platforms. A hand stand position is taken and the diver leans outward as if to start a Hand Stand dive, but just as he presses away with the hands, the body is tucked smartly and the feet and legs brought down between the platform and the upper body. In flight, the body comes upright and the diver shoots downward in an erect position to enter the water feet foremost.

Hand Stand with Forward Cut Through and One-half-Gainer. This is a really difficult dive done only from the ten meter platform by the most highly skilled divers. In this dive, the diver leaves from his hand stand position and cuts through with a little more force. Then, instead of taking the erect position, the head is inclined backward and the body slowly makes another half turn to enter head foremost as in a half-gainer. (See Fig. 67).

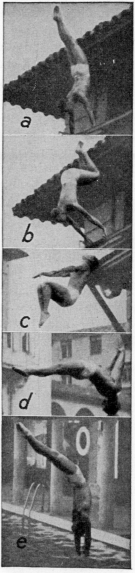

Fig. 67.—Hand stand with forward cut through and half-gainer.

Running Back Dive.—At first glance this may seem to be an impossible thing to accomplish yet it can be done by those who have mastered the normal running approach and some of the twist dives.

From a position at the base of the springboard the diver advances just as though he was making a regular running approach as he takes his hurdle leap to the tip of the board, he makes a half-turn in the air and lands ready to take off from a position facing inward. He then leaves the board and soars up and outward in a backward dive. This may be varied by going into a straight back somersault and (from the high board) a double backward somersault may be turned.

Running Spot Somersault and Dive.—When a diver has reached the point in his progress where he has achieved a high degree of knowledge of what he is doing at all times in all dives, he may under expert tutelage and instruction try this acrobatic feat. Before this can be tried on the board, however, the diver must have learned to do spotting backward somersaults on land. (A spot backward somersault is one in which the somersaulter turns in the air and lands on his feet squarely at the point from which he started.) On the board a "tumbling" belt may be used until the diver is sure of his whereabouts.

With a running approach, the diver hits the end of the board and leaps upward, turns a backward somersault and lands on his toes just back of the tip of the board. With the body leaning slightly forward he then takes the lift of the board once more and soars up and outward to do a plain front dive, a forward somersault, a forward one-and-one-half somersault, or a double forward somersault, depending upon his skill.

Flying Ring and Trapeze Diving

No one should attempt ring and trapeze diving until he has become a skilled fancy diver from the spring-board or unless he is an expert gymnast. These pieces of apparatus are not within the range of skill of the novice, so no easy learning methods are given nor are descriptions of the dives given. All of the dives are done, of course, at the end of the outward swing and away from the starting point.

All of the flying dives and all but two of the trapeze dives are done from a hanging or suspended position. The dives done facing outward correspond to the gainers in fancy diving or the "Flyaways" in gym-nastics. Thus, at the end of the forward swing the diver may let go and do a half-gainer, a full gainer or a double gainer. The dives done facing the take-off but always on the outward swing will correspond to the cutaway dives from boards and platforms. Thus, may be done a back swing, forward dive, a cutaway somersault, a cutaway somersault and a half and even a cutaway double somersault. The number of turns which can be taken will depend, of course, upon the length of the suspension lines and the range of the swing. Two dives may be done from a sitting posi-tion on the trapeze bar at the end of the forward swing. These are a plain front dive and a forward one-and-one-half somersault.

High Diving

High diving is a skill which has been developed almost entirely by the handful of professional men and women who make their living by exhibiting their prowess as high divers. From heights of sixty, seventy-five, a hundred, feet and more, they dive and somersault to thrill crowds of spectators at carnivals, fairs, and amusement parks. The "nerve" and skill they display in their diving feats command admiration but few indeed are those who seek to emulate them. High diving is hazardous in the extreme and its continued practice subjects the diver to physical punishment which cannot be anything but detrimental to the health in the long run.

The general run of swimmers should limit themselves to diving from much lower elevations. Fancy divers, however, who have become greatly skilled on boards and platforms may wish, on occasion, to try their skill from heights greater than the standard platforms. If their progress upward is regulated in steps of not more than ten feet, they can make adjustments in timing necessary for the greater heights. For plain dives, they will learn to leave the platform with the body angled upward, to allow for the turning of the body, due to the faster rate at which the head travels in downward flight. Somersaults (backward and gainer are the only reasonably safe ones) will be turned more slowly. Even the joy of such achievement, however, will not quite offset the unpleasant shock of the tremendous impact with the surface of the water. It will always be, even for the strongest and most compact physiques, painful in some degree.

In closing this section on fancy diving, it may be said that few divers have progressed very far alone and unaided in the many forms of fancy diving. To vie with others of like caliber and to strive to emulate those of greater ability are the most natural stimuli for development. A good teacher or coach is essential if the learner wishes to avoid the possibility of injury and to achieve the polish and grace in his diving which characterizes highly skilled performance.

INDEX

American crawl, history and description of, 137

Animal swimming, 3

Approach in diving, learning process for, 195
on diving board, 194

Armstrokes, general description of, 86
learning process for, 95
on back for beginner, 35
on front for beginner, 34
principles of, 51

Assyrian swimming, evidence of, 9

Australian crawl, history of, 137

Back crawl, description of, 130
learning process for, 133
use of arms in, 132
legs in, 132

Back dive, 204, 233
learning process for, 207
one-half twist, 245
pike, 233
running, 264

Back dives, diver facing the water, 240

Back double somersault dive, 236

Back glide, 30

Back header, 233
full twist, 245
one-half twist, 245

Back jackknife, dive, 214, 216, 237
full twist, 246
one-half twist, 246

Back one-and-one half somersault dive, 234

Back somersault, 211, 234
flying, 237
with full twist, 245
with one-half twist, 245

Back stroke, elementary, 100
learning process for, 103
European, mentioned, 116

Balance in swimming, 52

Basic swimming motions, 46

Beginner diving, 187

Beginner swimming skills, list of, 43

Beginner's stroke, on back, 38
on front, 36

Benjamin Franklin, first American authority on swimming, 12

Body position in swimming, 52

Breast stroke, butterfly, 167
evolution of, 11
history and full description of, 104
inverted, history and description of, 114
learning process for, 113
use of arms in, 95
variation of, 167

Breast stroke kick, description of, 85
use of, in treading water, 151

Breath holding, 19
in underwater swimming, 162

Breathing, principles of, in swimming, 54

Buoyancy, test of, to determine floating ability, 62

   use of in beginner floating, 22

   in swimming, 48

Butterfly breast stroke, 167

Butterfly dive, 226

Cannon ball dive, 229

Changing direction for beginner, 40

Cocoa-matting, 255

Combined stroke, on back for beginner, 38

   on front for beginner, 36

Co-ordination, principles of in swimming, 58

Crawl, back or inverted, description of, 130

   breathing in, 142

   co-ordination of, 141

   history and description of, 133

   legless, 172

   use of arms in, 140

Cutaway, double somersault, 239

   one-and-one-half somersault, 238

   somersault, 238

Deep diving, 163

Deep swimming, 163

Depths under diving boards and platforms, minimum for safety, 246

Dive, learning how to, 187

Diving, acrobatic, origin of, 180

   deep, 163

   form in the air, 196

   fundamentals of, 183

   general definition of, 178

   history of, 179

Diving, acrobatic, plain, 187

   position for feet foremost entry in, 186

   of hands in, 185

   pre-history of, 179

   safety in, 184

   safety principles of, 197

   sense, 201

   value of, 181

Diving boards, covering for, 255

   general description of, 250

   minimum depths under, standard heights for, 249

   mounting of, 252

Diving equipment, 246

   care and maintenance of, 255

   general information on, 257

Diving platforms, general description of, 254

   standard heights for, 249

Dog-paddle, description of arm-stroke in, 34

Double gainer somersault, 241

Double Mollberg somersault, 241

Double somersault, backward, 236

   forward, 230

Dutchman dives (see gainer and half-gainer), 240

Ears, pressure on, in deep diving, 166

Elementary back stroke, history and full description of, 100

Elementary turn for c l o s e d courses, 174

Elements of swimming, 45

Entering the water, for learning swimmers, 16

Etonian plunge, 228

European back stroke, mentioned, 116
Evolution of speed strokes in United States, 13

Fancy dives, 225
Fancy diving, fundamentals of, 202
  general, 200
Feet foremost surface dive, 157
Finning, description of, 35
First play activities in learning how to swim, 17
Float, inability to, 67
Floaters, classification of, 61
Floating, balanced, 63
  fundamentals of, 59
  horizontal, 62
  learning process for beginner, 23
  vertical or suspended, 66
Floating position, resting in for non-floaters, 68
Flutter kick, description of, 79
Flying backward somersault dive, 237
Flying dutchman, 218
Flying dutchman somersault (see full gainer), 240
Flying forward somersault, 231
Flying ring diving, 265
Flying rings for diving, 257
Form, diving, in air, 196
Forward dives, diver facing board, 237
  water, 225
Forward double somersault, 230
Forward one-and-one-half somersault, one-half twist, 244
Forward roll and dive, 262
Forward somersault, 208, 229
  flying, 231

Front dive, full twist, 243
  one-half twist, 213, 241
  running, 192
  standing, 191
Front jackknife, dive, 202, 228
  full twist, 243
  half-twist, 243
Full gainer somersault, 240
Full twist backward, 245
  forward, 243
Full twisting forward one-and-one-half somersaults, 244
Fundamentals of swimming, 47

Gainer somersault, 240
  double, 241
Gainer-and-a-half, 241
Getting adjusted to water, 17
Glide, importance of, in swimming, 59
Gliding, beginners, 29, 30

Half-gainer, 218
  one-half twist, 246
  piked, 240
Half-twisting backward one-and-one-half somersaults, 245
Hand stand, 260
  back fall, 261
  cut through, 263
  and half-gainer, 263
  forward somersault, 262
Hand-over-hand stroke, as used by Greeks and Romans, 10
  use of arms in, 94
Handspring dive, 260
Head stand, back fall, 260
High diving, 265
History of swimming, 7
Human stroke, 7, 36

Indian stroke, 9
Inverted side stroke, 169
Isander, 218

Jackknife surface dive, 153
Jelly fish float, 26
Jumping from height, feet fore-
most, 199

Kick glide, on back, 34
on front, 32

Leaping feet foremost from
height, 199
Learning how to swim, 15
Leg stroke for beginner, on back,
34
on front, 33
Leg strokes, learning method for,
86
principles of, 51
Levelling off from vertical,
beginner, 41
List of skills for beginner swimming, 43

Mercury dive, 258
Mollberg somersault, 240

Nose clip, use of, 165

One-and-one-half forward somer-
sault, 230
One-and-one-half gainer somer-
sault, 241
One-and-one-half Mollberg som-
ersault, 241
One-half twist dive, 241
Overarm side stroke, 121

Perfect swimmer, definition of,
147
Pike back dive, 233

Pike forward dive, feet foremost,
228
Pike half-gainer, 240
Pike Isander, 240
Plunge dive, 226
Pre-history of swimming, 5
Pressure under water, 163
Prone floating, 25
Prone glide, 29
Propulsion, first steps in, 29
fundamental principles of, in
swimming, 49

Quick surface dive, 156

Recovery of footing, from back
glide, 31
from prone position, 29
Relaxation, importance of, in
swimming, 53
Reverse scissors (see inverted
side stroke), 169
Rhythmic breathing, learning
process for, 20
Rocker dive, 259
Running front dive, 192
Running front header from
springboard, 193

Safety for beginning swimmer, 15
Sailor dive, 226
Scissors kick, inverted, 169
standard, description of,
75
use of in treading water, 151
Sculling, 69
Seal dive, 259
with jackknife, 259
Searching for objects under
water, 162
Seeing under water, 21
Shallow arm pull, 169

Side stroke, description and history of, 117
    inverted, 169
    learning process for, 120
    overarm, description and history of, 121
        learning method for, 126
    use of arms in, 87
Sideward dive, 258
Sitting jump, 229
Soldier dive, 226
Spanker dive, 261
Speed strokes, evolution of, 13
Spotter somersault and dive, 264
Springboard diving, 192
Springboards, box type, 256
    general description of, 250
    mounting of, 252
Standing front dive, 191
Standing-sitting, back somersault, 262
Standing-sitting dive, 261
Standing-sitting-standing dive, 262
Straight arm recovery in crawl strokes, 172
Strokes, classification of, according to movements, 99
Styles of swimming, 98
Surface dive, feet foremost, 157
    tuck form, 153
    using jackknife, 153

Surface diving, 152
Swallow dive, 226
Swan dive, 225
Swimming, deep, 163
    underwater, 159

Trapeze diving, 265
Trapeze, for diving, 257
Treading water, 149
Trudgen, learning process for, 130
Trudgen stroke, history and description of, 127
Trudgen-crawl, description of, 144
Tuck surface dive, 153
Turning in closed courses, 174
Turning over, for beginner, 40
Turtle dive, 259
Twist dive, 241
Two-and-one-half forward somersault dive, 231

Underwater swimming, 159
Upright swimming, reference to, 149
Useful variations of strokes, 166

Versatility of man in water, 3

Watermelon dive (see sitting jump), 229